What Reviewers H

In just a hundred pages Steve Kellmeyer distills the rich and complex 'Theology of the Body.' *Sex and the Sacred City* is a masterpiece of clarity. It's size, stylistic grace as well as it's logic should guarantee this book wide readership. Rarely is such a dense topic so delightfully explained and for adults as well as adolescents at that!
- **Al Kresta**, President-CEO Ave Maria Radio

Steve Kellmeyer is the author of Sex and the Sacred City, a great little book on John Paul's Theology of the Body. He is the pre-eminent expert I know of on issues of sexuality, marriage and the Church.
-**Tim Johnson**, editor of *Catholic Maniacs*

THANK YOU for *Sex and the Sacred City*. I LOVE IT! I have been using it with some patients and have been promoting it in my speaking. You did a great job making the Theology of the Body applicable to everyday life. What a gift you are to the Church. May God bless you.
- **Lisa Klewicki**, Ph.D.,
    Institute for Psychological Sciences, Arlington, VA

Surely it is not without significance that the pope who gave us the ground breaking 'Theology of the Body' over 129 general audiences visited 129 countries in his pontificate. This teaching is truly a message of hope and redemption for a despairing, fractured world. Steve Kellmeyer provides unprecedented access to this life-giving vision of human relationships imaging the mind-blowing love of the Blessed Trinity and the Church as the Mystical Body of Christ. Take a deep breath and see the gift of creation in a new and exciting way.
- **Edmund Adamus**,
    Director for Pastoral Affairs,
    Westminster Diocese, England

NEXT....

George Weigel has called the Theology of the Body "a theological timebomb set to go off." Steve Kellmeyer's *Sex and the Sacred City* is the first concussion from the explosion. A fine piece of work!
- **Mark P. Shea,**
Making Senses Out of Scripture and *By What Authority?*

Sex and the Sacred City really is a concise little treasure about a huge and epochal ('old but ever new') development/re-discovery in Christian theology...
-**Debra Murphy**, book reviewer

Our Holy Father has given humanity a masterpiece for understanding our true nature and dignity as sexual beings made in the image and likeness of God. Because of its complexity, most of us must piece together this teaching like a puzzle in order to fully appreciate its beauty. Steve Kellmeyer's *Sex and the Sacred City* is a marvelous tool to help us understand how the pieces of the puzzle go together.
- **Greg Schleppenbach**, State Director of the Nebraska Catholic Bishops' Pastoral Plan for Pro-Life Activities

The deep and philosophical thinking of our beloved Holy Father John Paul the Great is often hard to assimilate for us children of God with our feet of clay.

In his book *Sex and the Sacred City* Steve Kellmeyer has clarified in a remarkably comprehensible and unambiguous way just how precious is the gift we have received from God in letting us participate in His creative act. I hope very much that young people will read this book. They will then understand that a gift of this kind cannot be lightly given away or allowed to deteriorate.
- **Elizabeth Drucka Lubecka de Séjournet**
President, "Family, Hope for Tomorrow" Foundation

Engaged couples faces lit up when I started using Kellmeyer's *Sex and the Sacred City* with them. They desire the goodness and beauty of marriage as he explained it. Steve writes in a way that is easily understandable and desirable, as one would hear instruction from the very lap of our Blessed Mother.

It is a joy to witness the "light" spring forth from these couples; they desire this intimacy, a yearning to live out their faith wholeheartedly in their lives, and their eagerness to impart their faith to their children. Their eyes open, in deeper appreciation for the vocation of marriage, and a profound gratitude for their priests, and the priestly vocation. It is my hope that by using *SSC*, we will begin to change our culture of death to a culture of life and love. Thank you, Steve, for your gift of writing, compassion, and joy in explaining Theology of the Body in *Sex & the Sacred City*.

> - **Mamie Farish,**
> FertilityCare Practitioner, Los Alamos FertilityCare

It is awesome. Perfect for high school and college students, perfect for pre-Cana classes (it is all anyone would need for Pre-Cana except good luck and a good choice).

> - **Roxanne Shento**, book reviewer

First of all, I wanted to say thanks for the preview of *Sex and the Sacred City*. I liked it so much that we're making it one of the textbooks for our Vocations class next year. What a concise, powerful reflection on Theology of the Body!

> - **Kevin Kiefer**, assistant principal
> Blessed Trinity Catholic High School, Roswell, GA

NEXT....

The book is phenomenal!!... What differentiates Kellmeyer from West is his style, frequently charming and extremely easy to follow prose, and his willingness to take from other sources in addition to Pope John Paul II, including St. Thomas Aquinas and Popes Pius XI and Paul VI.

- **Maria van den Bosch**, book reviewer

I would like to say congratulations on a well-written and succinct book explaining Pope John Paul II's Theology of the Body in practical terms. I like the study guide approach, as well.

- **Nancy Brown**, book reviewer

Sex and the

Sacred City

Sex and the
Sacred City

Meditations on the *Theology of the Body*

Steven Kellmeyer

Bridegroom Press   Peoria, IL

"This book does not fall primarily within the theological realm which would be auxiliary to catechetics. Therefore it does not require or warrant the *Nihil Obstat* and *Imprimatur*. I have pursued it, however, and find that it is certainly free from theological error. I hope that it is used in ways which would be fruitful to those who purchase it."
Monsignor Steven P. Rohlfs, S.T.D.
Vicar General/Censor Librorum, Diocese of Peoria
July 21, 2004

Msgr. Rohlfs is now Rector of Mt. St. Mary's Seminary in Emmitsburg, Maryland.

Copyright 2003 by Steven Kellmeyer
ISBN: 0-9718128-1-0

Printed in the U.S.A.

Bridegroom Press
PO Box 96, Peoria, IL 61650
www.bridegroompress.com
E-mail: info@bridegroompress.com
Phone : 309-685-4085

Meditations

Other books by Steve Kellmeyer:

Bible Basics: A Scriptural Explanation of Catholic Faith
The Flesh of God: A Study of the Infancy Narratives
Fact and Fiction in the Da Vinci Code
Effective Habits of the Five People You Meet in Heaven
Artfully Teaching the Faith
The Middle Earth Riddle Book
Designed to Fail: Catholic Education in America

Note to the Reader

We often hear the phrase "city of God." Only rarely does anyone explain what it means. This book is intended to help the reader understand the meaning of the phrase. An old rule of thumb amongst teachers is this: a student does not really understand a concept until that student can teach the concept to someone else. Similarly, students won't use a concept they don't really understand.

It is my strong desire that these meditations move beyond the intellectual and plunge you directly into the experience of your life. If this book doesn't change the way you see, respond and love every day, then this has been a waste of time for all concerned. For this reason, each chapter ends with study questions, Scripture verses and *Catechism of the Catholic Church* references. Each meditation is meant to provide a starting point, a place for you to begin to explore how the subject under meditation can change your life. Use the meditation, the end-of-chapter questions and the resources as a foundation, and build from there.

Taken together, the meditations and their resources provide more than enough material to launch you into a fresh, new perspective on the Catholic Faith.

If you have never been exposed to the Theology of the Body, then you have never seen anything like this in your life.

Introduction

What is the "theology of the body"? On September 5, 1979, the newly-installed Pope John Paul II began a series of weekly audiences on human sexuality. Over the course of the next five years, he delivered over 120 general audiences, each covering an aspect of the vision. These audiences present an in-depth, coherent Scriptural explanation of the mystery of marriage and human sexuality. The first series of twenty-three catecheses, or teachings, based on Matthew 19:4, were entitled Original Unity of Man and Woman. The second set, forty-one catecheses in length called Blessed are the Pure of Heart, were based on Matthew 5:28. The fifty catecheses entitled Theology of the Body, were centered on Mark 12:23, while the last sixteen addresses contained reflections on Humanae Vitae.

Though he finished the introduction in November, 1984, he clearly intended this to be the beginning of a much greater and deeper work. And so it is proving to be, for the theology of the body is one of the the the most comprehensive and powerful discussion of man ever brought forward for Christian contemplation. In this vision, God's divinely inspired Scripture brilliantly combines with the voluptuous understanding of the greatest mystics of Christian history to produce an incisively sensual and beautiful vision of the human person.

While the weekly audiences laid the necessary groundwork, any discussion of this vision that limits itself to those early weekly audiences necessarily falls short of the full vision. These papal addresses were not meant to encapsulate the whole of the Church's understanding, rather, they sketch the implicit theme that has guided the Church in understanding God and herself for twenty-one centuries. This work, therefore, provides a brief overview not just of those weekly audiences, but of the whole grand sweep of Catholic theology in light of these audiences. The Holy Father's synthesis is the lens through which all Catholic teaching comes into twenty-first century focus. Today, we need to put on these eyes of the Church to see the beauty Who is God.

In every age, God has brought forward the weapons necessary to combat error. In this age, the most pernicious error revolves around a true understanding of human sexuality. Through the foundational synthesis provided by Pope John Paul II, we have been given the tools necessary to change the fabric of the culture. George Weigel has called this perspective "a theological time-bomb" set to go off, and so it is. Though the meditations contained in these pages may start slowly, they build towards a vision you have almost certainly never seen or heard before.

Prepare to be dazzled.

I. The Trinity

The revealed truth concerning man as 'the image and likeness' of God constitutes the immutable *basis for all Christian anthropology.*
John Paul II
On the Dignity and Vocation of Women, #6.

Though John Paul II did not begin his Wednesday catecheses with the Trinity, we will begin here, if only because it is easier to meditate on the theology of the body if this groundwork is first laid. Thinking about the Trinity is one of the most difficult things a human being can do. As a consequence, this first chapter is easily the most difficult section to understand. However, it is also very necessary. We cannot understand how we are made in the image and likeness of God unless we know who God is and what He is like. We don't need to understand everything about God in order to see how we are like Him, but we do need to understand two things: what it means to say "God is love" and what the "interpenetration of Persons" is.

When asked to explain the Trinity, most people fall back on one of the models they learned as children: three leaves of a clover, ice-water-steam, three wicks of a candle, etc. These analogies are sufficient for a child, but they are not sufficient for an adult. Adults need a better, deeper understanding. Fortunately, adults are capable of realizing something that children cannot really grasp: the Trinity is a communion of persons, a family whose life is love. Scripture itself tells us this, "I bow my knee before the Father, from whom every family in heaven and on earth is named" (Ephesians 3:14-15).

What does this mean? It means my family - myself, my wife, my children – is a family only because we together somehow image the Trinity of Persons within the Godhead. Insofar as we don't live out the Trinitarian life between us, we aren't really a family, we're just a bunch of people living at the same address. Likewise, your family is a family because it in some way images the Trinity. My family, your family, all families draw their name, their being, from God. He is the First Family.

So, if my family draws its name from God, who is God? We know a few things about Him. First, we know God is Pure Existence. That is, He does not need anything beyond Himself. He preexists everything that is made. He even preexists time. In fact, He is the source of everything that exists, He holds all of creation in existence from moment to moment. Second, we know even before He called anything or anyone else into existence, God is love.

If we think about this for a moment, we immediately realize that these two facts are hard to reconcile. We say that in the timeless time before everything was called into existence, God is love. But how can this be? Love requires an object. It is nonsense to say "I am in love. I am not in love with anyone, I am just in love." We cannot be *in love* unless we have *someone* to love. Yet, prior to creation, when God existed by Himself, not needing anything else, God is love. How can this be? Who is He loving? Who is the object of His love?

These two ideas of the original divine solitude and divine love are hard to reconcile because we are finite and imperfect. We do not have a clear understanding of what it means to be infinite and perfect. Let us contemplate "infinite perfection" for a moment.

The most basic kind of perfection is existence. For instance, we can either think about having the perfect haircut or perfect teeth, or we can actually *have* a perfect haircut and perfect teeth. We can think about having the perfect spouse, or we can *have* the perfect spouse standing next to us. Obviously, it is more perfect to have the reality of perfection than simply to have thoughts about perfection. Existence is more perfect than nonexistence. Now, consider God the Father. He is all-knowing, which means He has a perfect knowledge of Himself. If His knowledge of Himself is perfect, then His self-knowledge must have His own existence. He does. We call Him God the Son. God the Son is the perfect self-knowledge of the Father. We aren't used to thinking about God the Son this way, but we can see traces of this in the Scriptures: "In the beginning was the Word" (John 1:1).

Since God the Son is everything that God the Father knows about Himself, God the Father must give the Son everything He is. When we consider God the Son in this way, we see that God the Father pours Himself out completely into God the Son, holding nothing of Himself back. The Son has always existed, but He has also always found His origin in the Father. As human beings, we aren't used to seeing such a thing, but it happens in the Godhead. We admit as much in the Creed every Sunday: God the Son is *"eternally begotten* of the Father, God from God, Light from Light, true God from true God, *begotten, not made*, one in being with the Father." In a sense, in this total gift that the Father makes of Himself to the Son, He "takes care of" everything the Son is and needs from all eternity to all eternity.

Now, we know from Scripture that what the Son sees the Father do, the Son Himself does also (John 5:19-23). So, the Son follows the Father's example and pours Himself out into the Father completely, holding nothing of Himself back. Remember, this is happening outside of time, so we cannot say that there was a time when the Father existed and the Son did not, or vice versa. The Father has always been God, He has always had perfect self-knowledge, so He has always had the Son, He has always poured Himself out into the Son. The Son has always done what the Father does, so He has always poured Himself out into the Father. This is called "the exchange of Persons" and it is a perfect exchange.

But wait – the exchange of persons within the Godhead is *perfect*. That means this complete outpouring of God the Father into God the Son, and the complete outpouring of God the Son into God the Father has His own existence as well. The perfect exchange of Divine Persons is Himself a Divine Person. He is God the Holy Spirit "who proceeds from the Father and the Son. With the Father and the Son He is worshipped and glorified." God the Father begets God the Son. The Father and the Son together "breathe" the Holy Spirit. You have heard a lover say of his beloved, "You are the air I breathe!" This is what the Father and the Son say of the Spirit. That is why a human person might say it about a person he loves - we know we must live out in ourselves the absolute reality of God, in whose image and likeness we are. Even people who don't believe in God or understand the Trinity understand what it means to speak in this way.

Now that we have explained this interaction, we should summarize it. Read this part slowly, to make sure it is understood. God the Father pours Himself out completely through God the Holy Spirit into God the Son. This means God the Father gives Himself completely away to God the Spirit and, at the same time, He gives Himself completely away to God the Son. Likewise, God the Son pours Himself out completely through God the Holy Spirit into God the Father. He gives Himself away completely to the Spirit with nothing left over and He gives Himself completely to the Father also. So, we are not surprised to see that God the Holy Spirit pours Himself out completely to God the Father, holding nothing of Himself back, but at the same time, God the Holy Spirit pours Himself out completely to God the Son in exactly the same way. This is why we say that Love is a Person, for the Holy Spirit is the Person Who is the love between the Father and the Son. This is how God exists in Himself. This is how God is love. This is one of the two things we need to understand.

The second thing we need to understand is the interpenetration of Persons. The following analogy is not perfect, but it will have to do. Imagine that I drew a huge circle and said that within the circle was contained everything that is God the Father. If you asked me where God the Son was in relationship to God the Father, I would have to draw a second circle inside the large one and label the second circle God the Son. The Holy Spirit would be yet another circle within the second – three concentric circles.

However, if I drew that first large circle and labeled it God the Son, and you asked me where God the Father was in relation to God the Son, then *within* the first circle I would draw a smaller one for the Father, and within the Father's circle, one for the Holy Spirit. The same would be true if the Holy Spirit were the outer circle – the other two Persons would be completely contained within. Each Person of the Trinity is completely contained within each of the other two Persons simultaneously, yet there is never any confusion of Persons, each Person is always distinct from the other two. This is called the interpenetration of Persons. It is rather confusing to picture, but we need not understand it completely. We need only recognize that the interpenetration of persons is true.

At this point, some distinctions need to be made. We have seen that God is three Persons, but what does this mean? What is a person? How is the one divine nature related to the three divine Persons?

"Nature" is a shorthand way of describing the range of activities and attributes that a being has. Something with a rabbit nature, for instance, has long ears, can hop after the manner of rabbits, and do other rabbit kind of things. Kangaroos, having a kangaroo nature, have kangaroo ears, can hop after the manner of kangaroos and do kangaroo things. Rocks, having only a rock nature, lack ears and cannot hop at all. Everything that exists has its own range of activities and way of being - this is its nature. When we use the word "nature," this is what we mean.

"Person," on the other hand, is a being which possesses an intellect and a will. "All right," I see you saying to yourself, "This may be well and good, but what is an intellect? What is a will?" The intellect is that which knows; the will is that which chooses. The will is sometimes called an "appetite" of the intellect (similar to "hunger" being an appetite of the stomach) because the will chooses based on the information supplied to it by the intellect. When we say a person is that which possesses an intellect and a will, we are saying that a person possesses the ability to know and choose. That is the essence of personhood. What a person can know and what a person can choose depends on what kind of nature the person possesses. An angel knows and can choose in a way different than human persons, for instance. The person's nature is the range of options available to the person's intellect and will.

So, we could summarize by saying "nature" is "what" and person is "who." The difference is easily demonstrated. Assume that you were outside on a dark night and you heard a rustle in the bushes. If upon hearing the rustle you ask "What is that?" you have asked a question about a thing's nature: "What is it that has the capacity to rustle bushes?" If you ask "Who is that?" you have asked a question about a person: "Who is it that knows bushes can be rustled, and chose to undertake an action which caused them to rustle?"

Every person possesses a nature, but not everything that has a nature is a person. Rabbits have a rabbit nature, but are not persons. Apes, giraffes, dolphins – all possess their own kind of natures, and have a specific range of actions, sometimes a large range of rather complex action, but none are persons.

Only three kinds of persons exist: Divine Persons, angelic persons, and human persons. The Divine Persons are uncreated. The one God who is the Divine Persons created everything else, including the other two kinds of persons.

Because there is only one God, only one divine nature exists. The divine nature is the divine intellect and the divine will. Now, a person is that which possesses an intellect and will. Since this is true, we know that God the Father possesses the one divine intellect and divine will – He does not share it with anyone, not even the Son or the Spirit. Similarly, the Son possesses the divine nature entirely to Himself, He does not share it with the Father or the Spirit. Likewise, the Spirit entirely possesses the one divine intellect and the one divine will, He does not share it with the Father or the Son. Each Person is fully God because each Person completely possesses the divine nature, yet there is only one God.

We don't know how He manages this. There is no analogy for it in our experience. I do not know with your intellect, you do not choose with my will. With God, it is different. What the Father knows, the Son and Spirit likewise know, for there is but one divine intellect. What the Son chooses, the Father and Spirit likewise choose, for there is but one divine will. There is never any opposition between Father, Son and Spirit, never any contention. All three Persons act together at all times, for He is one God with one intellect and one will.*

We call this a mystery, but we must be careful when we use that word. We tend to think the word "mystery" refers to something we don't know anything about. Actually, that isn't true. A mystery is something we know quite a lot about. A mystery is something we understand, we just don't understand it completely.

When we recognize truth, and then realize this granite-ribbed truth is but the bare outline of a much larger truth, a truth that invites us to explore more deeply, we have encountered a mystery. In a murder mystery, for instance, we understand that someone has died, we understand that someone else caused the death, but we do not understand exactly how the death was caused or exactly who caused it. We see part of the truth, but not the whole of it.

In the scientific investigation of a natural mystery, we understand that a phenomenon occurs, we may know even know a lot about the effects it has on the world, but we do not understand exactly why or how it occurs. Again, we see a part, but not the whole.

In the case of the divine mystery, we understand there is only one divine intellect and one divine will, we understand each Person

---

* Thanks to Frank Sheed's marvelous work, *Theology for Beginners*, for the explanation of Trinity and nature contained here.

of the Trinity possesses it, but we don't completely understand *how* He does that. This mixture of knowing and not-knowing is what makes it a mystery, it is why we call the Trinity a mystery.

Now, as we begin to explore this mystery, the next statement is very important to understand. We know the only distinction between the three Persons is in the relations: Father eternally begets Son, Son is eternally begotten of the Father, Father and Son together eternally "breathe" or spirate, the Spirit. Only relationship distinguishes the divine Persons. Nothing else.

What has all of this to do with us? Every created thing God has given us, from rocks through vegetation and animals, stars and planets, everything - including our own bodies and souls - is meant to help us understand Him. So, what do we know about God?

God is Three Persons in one God. Since each of the Three Persons own the single Divine Nature, each Person is distinguished from the other two only by His relationship to the other two. The Father begets the Son, the Son is begotten by the Father. The Father and Son together breathe forth the Spirit, the Spirit is breathed forth by the Father and the Son. Since we are made in God's image and likeness, and since the Divine Persons are distinguished only by their relationships, we can see that our own personhood depends crucially on our relationships with other persons - human, angelic and Divine. In fact, by having studied how the Persons of the Godhead are distinguished, we can now see that our relationships are necessarily integral to what defines each of us as persons. In a certain sense, there is no such thing as a person who is in complete solitude. Indeed, one can make the argument that our personhood exists - that we are persons - only and precisely because of the relationship we are called into with God and with one another.

Because relationship is necessary to being a person, we know that no person can be an object - each of us is a subject. What is the difference? Consider how subject and object operate in a sentence. The subject of the sentence is the actor, the one who has many options for behavior, and is free to choose among them. The object of the sentence has no such freedom; he must accept what the subject chooses. The object's behavior is limited by the action of the subject; the subject doesn't necessarily have to think about the object, or understand much about him, or care about him at all.*

Considered in that light, it is clear why a person is never an object. Each human being is a "who" and never just a "what." My contemplation of myself does not define my personhood; rather, a crucial part of what defines the personhood of each one of us is our contemplation and treatment of one another: man, angel and, most especially, God. The shattering implications of this single fact will color everything that follows.

This is the beginning of our meditation. We now know something about both ourselves and God that we had not known before. So, now that we have grasped a few essentials about God, we can begin to discover how these essentials affect us, who are made in His image and likeness.

---

* Thanks to Jenice Greb for this marvelous description.

Questions for discussion:
1) Compare and contrast what you knew about Trinity before reading this chapter and after reading this chapter. What has changed?

2) While discussion of "the interpenetration of persons," also known as *circumincession* or *perichoresis*, was common in the writings of early Christians like St. Gregory Nazianzen, it is hardly ever talked about today. Why do you think today's Christians no longer know or talk about this aspect of God?

3) Now that you know how the First Family lives, what implications does this have for how your own family is meant to live? What implications does it have for how the family of man is supposed to live?

Scriptures for Contemplation
Eph 3:14-19 - Family and fullness of God
Deut 6:4-5 and Gen 1:26 - Solitude and company
1 John 4:13-15 and John 14:16-26 - Spirit, Son and Father

Catechism of the Catholic Church
Read and consider articles #232-267

II. Creation

> By coming to restore the original order of creation
> disturbed by sin, he himself gives the strength and grace to
> live marriage in the new dimension of the Reign of God.
>
> *Catechism of the Catholic Church,* #1615

As we discussed above, God did not need to create. He is perfect in Himself, living a life of overflowing love. He *chose* to create. One of the greatest minds of the Church, St. Thomas Aquinas, said, "The key of love opened the hand of God and creation sprang forth."

His intention is to create beings like unto Himself, so they may share in the endless joy of love that He is. Now, God is pure spirit. He does not have a body. Angels image God; they are also pure spirit, like God. Like God, they do not grow in knowledge, instead, they are created already knowing all they need to know for all eternity. Like God, they have perfect knowledge of the consequences of their actions. Unlike God, however, their knowledge is vast, but finite.

At the moment of individual creation, each angel was given a choice: love God or refuse to love Him. When given the choice to participate in God's life of love, many chose to do so, but some chose against. In both cases, every angel knew full well the consequences of his choice. Even now, we could give them no new information that would change their minds. That is why the angels who chose not to participate in God's life of love, that is, the fallen angels, will never repent. They have always known everything they needed to know. They made their choice. In this sense, they also image God.

Thus it was with the angels, but when God created Adam and Eve, He created them to image Him in a different way. Instead of making human persons pure spirit - as He did the angels - He combined man's immortal spirit with a material body. The immortal spirit which gives life to the human body is the human soul. The human soul is the human intellect and human will.

In creating Adam and Eve, He created and simultaneously united immortal spirit to material body, which became a human body as a result. Adam's soul was united to his body in a bond that was meant to be indissoluble. Understanding the consequence of this unity is crucial. We are bodies just as much as we are souls. However, since material bodies grow and mature over time, He created our intellect and will in such a way that our soul's ability to realize its full capacities grows and matures over time as well. Human beings, then, are made to grow and mature in a way that angels are not. God does not change, but we do, we can, and we are meant to.

Thus, when God created Adam, Adam recognized that he was like God in his own original solitude, but he also recognized that his original solitude was not like God's. Something was missing. He could not experience the communion of persons as God does. Though he sought throughout creation, none of the other creatures was a suitable partner for him. In his very being he appealed to God, asking Him to remedy the lack. God rewarded all mankind in Adam by making us even more like Himself. He created Eve.

Mankind is not complete without woman. We have often heard this, but we are now in a position to see why it is true. Each Person of the Trinity pours Himself out into an equal - into Someone who possesses the very divine nature He Himself possesses. Since Adam alone possessed human nature prior to Eve's creation, he was, in a certain sense, not able to express the fullness of his human personhood. He had no equal to serve, no human person to be in relationship with, no one to pour himself out into.

This is what we mean when we say Adam and Eve were made for each other: each was made in God's image, each was made to experience the communion of persons. Without woman, man would be, in a certain sense, barely recognizable. With woman as his equal partner, man and woman are together like unto God. This was a source of incredible joy for both.

The ecstasy of the personal communion Adam and Eve experienced in their primordial marriage can be found in Scripture's very first reference to Eve. The Hebrew that describes Adam's "deep sleep" translates into Greek as *ekstasis*: "ecstasy." Similarly, the Sumerian symbol for "rib" and "life" coincide. Thus, Scripture tells us that Eve is the cause of Adam's ecstasy, and for her part, she finds her life in him. Father and Son, Adam and Eve: the second each finding origin in the first but always coequal as persons to the first. Just as Father and Son interpenetrate persons, so Adam and Eve began to live out the interpenetration of persons in their own bodies, as they were meant to, for, from the beginning, God instituted the one-body union. Communing together in their solitude, they lived a life of marvelous joy.

This marriage of body and soul, man and woman, is part of the gift of original holiness, given by God to mankind. This means Adam and Eve, in their immortal spirit-bodies, were created with all the grace they needed in order to be in perfectly harmonious communion with God and with each other.

Now we have introduced a new term, a term which needs definition: grace. What is grace? Grace is *power*. Grace is the life of God. It is the power to live as God lives. Like the angels before them, God called Adam and Eve into a higher union with Himself, to a much more intimate union. Because Adam and Eve were made to grow and mature, they were meant to come to this intimate union not through a once-for-all choice, like the angels, but through a maturing process, in which their grace-empowered choice would help them grow towards God like a vine grows towards the sun. Their understanding of Him would grow; their ability to choose Him would be strengthened at each step. God made them to share in His own divine nature; He called them to participate in the inner life of the Trinity.

He called them to this union through obedience – by being obedient to their Creator through refusing to eat of the fruit of a certain tree, Adam and Eve would acknowledge their total dependence on God. They would live out their real relationship with Him, and grow more fully and intimately able to commune with Him. Adam and Eve were made in the image and likeness of God Himself. They were made to share in the divine nature (2 Peter 1:3-4). They knew this was what they were made for. Through the power of original holiness, they had everything they needed in order to be elevated to the relationship God intended.

Now, in order to see what it means to "share in the divine nature," we first have to explain the phrase "image and likeness." What does it mean to say Adam and Eve were made in God's image and likeness? The "image" of God is personhood. Because Adam and Eve are persons, they image God. "Likeness" to God is having the power of God, that is, having grace. So, to say Adam and Eve were made in God's image and likeness is to say that Adam and Eve were made persons with a full complement of grace.

Since personhood depends on relationship and since grace is power, we can re-phrase this yet another way. Adam was given the divine ability to pour himself out totally to Eve, to serve her every need and care for her. Eve was likewise given the divine ability to pour herself out totally to Adam, to serve his every need and care for him. Together, both were to give themselves entirely to God. They were meant to live out the image and likeness of God in their own bodies. God told them to do so the instant He established them as a communion of persons.

God had created a fully-graced creation, a creation that was very good, and placed immortal persons in this creation to care for it. Man and woman were meant to do as He does. The gift of original holiness, this fullness of grace they had, was meant to be passed on to each succeeding generation of mankind through all the generations. Immediately after their creation, Adam and Eve were commanded to be fruitful and multiply (Genesis 1:28), to bring more immortal persons into existence, to serve and care for creation. God always intended all human beings to be fully graced, as Adam and Eve were. He also intended Adam and Eve to participate as He created more human, immortal persons. Indeed, right down to this day, He refuses to create more immortal human persons *unless* we participate with Him in that creation. He intended Adam and Eve to pass on not only life, but their gifts of grace as an inheritance to their children.

The power of that primordial grace is enormous: it held and holds all of creation in existence. The grace of creation prior to the Fall was the grace of marriage. Specifically, it was the grace which kept several harmonies, or "marriages," in existence. The first of the marriages is that of the intellect and will. The grace of original holiness empowers the capacities of the intellect and will. With the power of grace, Adam and Eve's intellects could clearly perceive the good and their wills could perfectly choose the good that the intellect discovered.

The power of this grace also accomplished the second marriage, the marriage that indissolubly unites soul and body. In regard to this union, St. Hilary of Poitiers once remarked "The bridegroom and the bride represent our Lord God in the body, for the flesh is the bride of the spirit." What does this mean? We know the human soul is the form of the human body. What does it mean to say this?

Consider what happens when someone makes Jell-O. The Jell-O liquid is poured into the Jell-O mold so that the liquid fills the mold in every crack and crevice. It takes on the form of the mold. Once it has spent a few hours in the refrigerator, the Jell-O can actually be popped out of the mold and still retain the form of the mold. What was previously shapeless goo is now in the shape of a giraffe or rabbit. However, if the Jell-O is popped out of the mold and left to sit on the table overnight, it will revert to its previous form: shapeless goo.

In the same way, our immortal souls wrap around and shape every cell of our bodies. Our souls form our bodies. As long as soul is united to body, the body retains its shape and its life. But, if ever the soul were to be separated from the body, the body would disintegrate just as the Jell-O does. This separation of soul and body has never been part of God's plan. God intended soul and body to be indissolubly united. What God has joined, no man should attempt to separate.

The third marriage is the marriage of man and woman. The power of this grace puts man and woman in proper relationship to one another. Man has headship over woman, woman stands by man. Now, O gentle reader, I can see the steam rising from you as you contemplate the terrible misogyny of the previous sentence. Do not fear. "Headship" does not mean what you might assume.

When we are describing an interaction between persons, "headship" or authority of one person over another person is based in total self-giving service. Consider the Person of God the Father, who has authority over God the Son. Indeed, God the Son will say His own authority comes not from Himself, but comes rather from the Father (see John 5:27-30, 8:27, 12:49, 14:10). Similarly, the Spirit's authority comes from the Father (John 16:13). Why is God the Father the source of authority? Because the Father pours Himself completely into the Son and completely into the Spirit; He is the origin of the Son and the Spirit (*Catechism of the Catholic Church*, #245). He is, in a sense, taking care of, serving, the Son and Spirit through all eternity. Thus, though each Person of the Trinity is coequal in divine nature and power, still the Father has a certain headship over the Son and the Spirit.

In the same way, the authority of man in relationship to woman derives entirely from his loving service to her needs, his gift of himself entirely to her. Man's care for woman, his service to her, his actions on her behalf, this is his authority. Insofar as he does not do these things, he has no authority over woman whatsoever. The text of Ephesians 5 is radically linked to Genesis 1 and 2. Paul will say that husband and wife should submit to one another precisely because he recognizes this reality. Though man and woman are coequal in nature and dignity before God, man is meant to give his life for woman, woman is meant to be loved by man.

These three "marriages" of intellect-will, soul-body, and man-woman was not all that God gave, however. The power of this primordial grace also gave mankind authority over creation. Though this relationship is more a harmony than it is a marriage, still it is the case that mankind has control and responsibility, that is, mankind has stewardship over creation. All created things exist to serve him. He has a duty to make sure that nothing in creation is misused.

The power of the grace of original holiness was intended to lead man into the greatest marriage of all: man's participation in the divine nature. This is, in fact, the whole purpose of every other aspect of man's existence and even the whole purpose of the created universe: everything was designed to lead Adam, Eve and their descendants into the most intimate relationship with God. While human persons would not possess the divine nature as the Persons of the Trinity do, we were all intended to become sharers in it and intimate members of the family of Persons who is the one God.

Now, before we go on, we must notice something very important. Grace can be described in many ways. Grace is power. Grace is the indwelling of the Trinity. Grace is the very life of God. But in the created order, grace is meant to establish and maintain marriages. Intellect and will are "married" together, with intellect having a certain headship over the will. Soul and body are married together, with the soul having headship over the body. Man and woman are married together, with man having a headship of service towards woman. Mankind and creation are harmoniously bound together, with mankind having headship over creation. God intends man to be married to Himself, and He has headship over us. The entirety of Genesis 1 and 2, indeed, the whole of Scripture from beginning to end, is about marriage. Marriage is the primordial sacrament; God intends us to know Him through our experience of marriage. God intends us to know Him through our experience of love.

When we compare Adam and Eve's place in the created universe to God's, we begin to see the truth of Psalm 8, "What is man that thou art mindful of him, the son of man that thou dost care for him? Yet thou hast made him little less than God, and dost crown him with glory and honor...."

Questions for discussion:
1) Compare and contrast what you knew about angels before reading this chapter and afterwards. What has changed?
2) How does the definition "grace is power" help your understanding of grace in our lives?
3) Given the explanation of headship here, how would you explain the relationship between the Church and Scripture?
4) How has this discussion enhanced your understanding of love?

Scriptures for Contemplation
Gen 1:28 and 2:18-25 - Original solitude and first blessing.
Gen 8:15-9:7 - Repetition of solitude and blessing
2 Pet 1:3-4 - Sharing in the divine nature
Matt 19:4-6 - Indissoluble marriage
Eph 5:21-33 - Marriage and headship

Catechism of the Catholic Church
Read and consider articles #325-384

III.   The Fall

Man is a person in the unity of his body and his spirit.
The body can never be reduced to mere matter. It is a
spiritualized body, just as man's spirit is so closely united
to the body that he can be described as an embodied spirit.
John Paul II
A Letter to Families, #19

Spirit is invisible, but body is visible. The visible, created world
is meant to inform us about the invisible world. You know who I
am because you see my body. You interact with me by interacting
with my body. My visible reality literally tells you about my spiritual
reality, for I do not communicate with you directly mind to mind,
but through the use of my created body and created things (air,
paper, ink, etc.). God has always intended it to be so.

Just as God joined body and soul in Adam, and joined Adam
to Eve, so God intended to join Himself, give Himself, to both
Adam and Eve. However, as we have seen, Adam and Eve were
made to grow and mature. Thus, we know God also intended a time
of preparation so that they could be made ready for the fullness
of this union.

Prior to the Fall, Adam and Eve had a good understanding of
what was coming. They could talk with God face to face in the cool
of the morning, and experience every day in the joys of the Garden
and the interpenetration of their own bodies the marvelous things
God had given them. They were naked without shame, for Adam
knew how to love his spouse totally and always did so, perfectly
giving himself to her and serving her in every way. Eve, seeing
what Adam did for her, did the same for him. They were meant

to be fruitful and multiply, and they knew it. It is certain that the most marvelous thing Adam and Eve experienced, apart from their increasingly intimate communion with the Persons of the one God, was their intimate communion with each other's persons. The gift of sexual union, the interpenetration of their human persons in a total gift of self to other, was the delicious foretaste of the delightful full communion with the Divine Persons that they knew was coming. The gift they made of themselves to one another as they awaited most intimate communion with the divine allowed them to live out all they knew of God in their own bodies.

However, if we say the first couple experienced sexual union prior to the Fall, we must answer an important question. Since God commanded Adam and Eve to be fruitful and multiply, we must ask why He did not bless them with children prior to the Fall. We can see the possible outlines of an answer in the fact that human persons are meant to grow and mature.

When we contemplate the divine interpenetration of Persons, we see that the sexual act is a lived expression of the inner life of the Trinity. Yet, though Adam and Eve become one flesh, the interpenetration is not total – Adam is not completely contained within Eve, nor Eve within Adam. Just as they were in close communion but not yet in total intimacy with the Godhead, so their bodies are in one-flesh union, but do not totally interpenetrate.

Remember, God intended Adam and Eve to grow more fully towards Him; they had to learn and live obedience to every one of His commands. In completing this process, they would be divinized. That is, though they would not possess the divine nature as He does, God would bring them to share in His own divine nature. As a result, they would live out the greatest and most splendid intimacy in their own bodies. Their sexual ecstasy would produce the greatest ecstasy of all – the ecstasy of co-creation in new immortal life, a new living image of the Godhead, a child who would completely interpenetrate Adam's greatest joy and be completely contained within her, the person of Eve. Children were to come as a result of attaining full, intimate communion with the Divine Persons. In pregnancy, the visible would signify the invisible, human flesh would signify the total interpenetration of persons found in the Trinity.

Sadly, instead of growing towards God, Adam and Eve were beguiled by Satan. He convinced them that God did not really intend to give Himself to them, that He did not really intend to share His life with them, He did not really intend to allow them to participate in the divine nature. Satan convinced Adam and Eve that the only hope they had to attain a share in divinity was to disobey God and strike out on their own. Remember, God had made them for this supernatural end, sharing in the divine nature. This was the purpose of the whole of creation and Adam and Eve knew it. But, Satan led them to believe God could not be trusted. If they would be as gods they would have to do it on their own. As a result, the first couple chose to be disobedient. By this very act, they essentially reached inside of themselves, scooped out the inheritance of power/grace given to them, threw it away, and said to God, "We don't *want* to be like you, God. We will do it our way."

Though they were intended to grow in knowledge, the Fall was for Adam and Eve a crisis of knowledge. It was a crisis of faith, hope, and love, the three greatest virtues, each of which can be seen as a way of knowing, a form of knowledge.

Faith is another word for trust. Trust is a kind of knowledge. If I need a good car mechanic, and I trusted you to know one, I would accept whoever you recommended, even if I had never met him. This is what it means to say "Faith is the evidence of things not seen" (Hebrews 11:1). *You* are the evidence. I don't trust the mechanic because I have seen him work; rather I trust the mechanic because you recommended him, and I know you are trustworthy.

With God, this trust is two things at once. When God reveals Himself to me through the natural world He has created for my comfort and care, He reveals Himself as trustworthy. When He reveals Himself to me, His revelation gives me the power to trust Him. So Faith is both the sure knowledge that God is trustworthy and it is the power to trust Him absolutely.

Likewise, Hope is also a kind of knowledge. Where Faith is knowledge in the trustworthiness of the messenger, in this case, God, Hope springs from knowledge of the message. God promises me Himself. Because I have Faith in God, when He speaks to me of His promises and His Love, I have Hope. Hope is a consequence of Faith.

Love is a knowledge far greater than either. Love is fully living out the message of hope given by the one you trust completely. It is the power to live in absolute intimacy with the one you know and trust, the one who gives you Hope. While Faith is the evidence of things not seen, Love is standing before God completely revealed to Him, and He completely revealed to me. It is the experience of the bride and the bridegroom on their wedding night, the experience of Adam and Eve, who were each naked in the other's gaze and were not ashamed. It is Adam and Eve, living out their love in each other's arms, in the sight of God.

Just as the soul is the form of the body, so Love is the form of Faith and Hope. It wraps around and holds together Faith and

Hope. Adam served the woman who was so eminently worthy of his service. The very act of service constantly re-affirmed the fact that she was trustworthy. The hope she gave him, each day's joy, was superseded only by the promise of the next day's even greater joy.

But in the test, Adam and Eve each betrayed the other. Adam - who was to live his life in constant service to Eve - failed to protect her from the presence of the serpent. Eve - who was to live her life in constant service to Adam - failed to protect him from an act of disobedience. Ultimately, they were not willing to give themselves, to trust themselves, completely to God. They threw away their trust in God, threw away their belief in His promises, lost their ability to live His life.

This is the Fall. Remember, each person of the Godhead gives Himself completely away. Every human person is called to live that way and, in Adam and Eve, we were given the power to do it, but we refused it. We threw away the power. We no longer had the grace, the power, to give to our children. Thus, we are now conceived without the power we need to do what it is God made us to do. This lack of power, this lack of grace, is original sin.

Many Christians think the first couple's decision to have sex caused the Fall, because they see that Adam and Eve were ashamed of their nakedness after the Fall. Yet, if we look at Genesis 1, we see that the first blessing/command given to the new couple was "Be fruitful and multiply, fill the earth and subdue it." God commanded them to procreate. Rather than being the cause of our curse, our sexuality is our first and one of our greatest natural blessings. God blessed us with the ability and desire to have sex in the beginning, in Genesis 1, when all things were created good. We don't fall from this state of unashamed nakedness until Genesis 3.

So why did Adam and Eve feel shame at their nakedness after the Fall? After all, they were naked before the Fall as well. What had changed?

C. S. Lewis once pointed out that if we had the eyes to really see a human person who had been transformed by grace, we would strongly be tempted to fall down and worship. Prior to the the Fall, Adam and Eve understood that. In the Fall, we lost that power. Before the Fall they had been clothed in the power of grace. That grace had given them powerful knowledge, powerful wills, powerful perceptions. Now they were stripped of that power. Before they had known how to make a gift of themselves, each to the other. Now the power to fully know how to do this was gone. Adam could no longer make a complete gift of himself to Eve. Worse, in his new blindness, he began to see her as an object instead of a glorious person. For Eve, the same was true; Adam began to be an object. Persons are worthy of love. Objects are worthy only of use. Each now carried a tendency to want to use the other. They knew this tendency was wrong. They were ashamed of it.

Each had stopped serving the other. In failing to live that life of total service to the other, the "soul" of their relationship (love) had been separated from the "body" (bodily expressions of that love), the form had been separated from the substance. Since they had broken service to one another, they had broken trust with one another. Neither could trust the other to catch him when he fell, or her when she fell. When they lost faith in God, they found that they had lost faith in each other as well.

As Faith crumbled, Hope crumbled with it. Now they could not totally trust the other's promises. The knowledge was no longer sure, the power to live it was no longer present.

They hid from God because their insufficient Faith meant that they did not know what He would do. They hid from each other their ability to be like God, because the divine power was no longer something they could trust; it would now be something that they feared. God is life, the wellspring of life. Adam and Eve hid the wellsprings of human life behind fig leaves. God confirmed their instinct to veil the flesh by giving them clothes of animal skin. They had moved from total love, total service, to a service tinged with self-interest, with lust. Because each was now blind, they could not allow themselves to be seen.

God's gift is the gift of living like Him in our own bodies. Each of the Three Persons of the Trinity gives Himself entirely to each of the other Two Persons. Because we are in the image and likeness of God, human persons live in harmony only through this same kind of mutual self-giving. Love desires the other's good through the gift of self. Love requires self-sacrifice, self-donation. Lust, on the other hand, is self-centered. It desires my short-term good through the use or, if necessary, the abuse of another. They discovered the oldest of truths: the opposite of love is not hate, the opposite of love, of service, is use. Using the other person like an object instead of serving the other person as an image of service to God - that is the sin of the Fall.

In disobeying God, both Adam and Eve recognized that they had the power to use the other like an object, the power to abuse the other. Adam harmed his wife by failing to protect her from the serpent. Eve harmed Adam by giving him the fruit. Adam harmed Eve by repudiating her before God, "This woman who *YOU* gave me, *she* gave me the fruit to eat."

Their nakedness had turned from a gift of love into a threat of being used, the continuing threat of possible harm. They defended their nakedness by clothing it, hiding it. Because the effects of the Fall still run through every human relationship today, that defense remains crucial to the integrity of our relationships, to the integrity of ourselves as persons.

In the loss of grace that was the Fall, in our rebellion against God, all the marriages, all the harmonies, disintegrated. The power was gone. The intellect darkened and the will weakened. We can no longer fully know the good. Even when we do know the good, we are too weak to choose it on our own. Paul talks about this when he says, "For I do not do the good I want, but the evil I do not want is what I do" (Romans 2:19). The divorce between intellect and will is the weakness that permits sin.

Body now rebels against soul. When it succeeds in kicking the soul out of its domain, the body yells, "Victory!" and disintegrates into dust, for the soul, which is the body's life force, is gone. The divorce that we call death is precisely the separation of soul and body. Death is the first divorce mentioned in Scripture.

Man and woman are now in rebellion against one another. The curse of Genesis 3:16b, "he shall rule over you" is not a curse put by God upon man. It is simply God describing what the effects of losing grace will be. As the brilliant chastity speaker Jeremy Pitt-Payne notes, "Now, man does not serve woman, yet still unjustly demands to have authority over her: 'Woman, obey me!' The woman, who no longer supports the man, replies with the shout, 'Crucify him!'"

As man rebelled against God, so creation rebels against mankind. Prior to the Fall, Adam could safely walk in front of a hungry lion. His sons have no such surety. We rejected God's marriage proposal and threw away His gift. The whole created universe has not yet ceased to tremble from the shock.

All of us, all the children of Adam and Eve, lost our inheritance of grace. A true son or daughter has inheritance rights. We don't have an inheritance anymore. Where human beings had been rich, we now are born in graceless poverty, living a grubby existence on the wrong side of the railroad tracks. We are slaves now to sin. We call this poverty of grace original sin. Like a collapsible water jug with the water drained out, this loss of grace caused our human nature to collapse upon itself. Yet, though we are desperately harmed by the loss, we are not totally corrupted. God made all things good. We are no longer conceived with the full power of grace we were originally intended to have, and we certainly don't have grace sufficient to attain any of the proper harmonies on our own, but, as the Scripture reminds us, God's grace springs new every morning (Lamentations 3:22-23). We still have within us some small spark of the original goodness God gave us at the beginning.

As with all kinds of sin, original sin does not really have its own existence. Evil, sin, both are a lack of something – a lack of grace. God created all things good. Evil is the result of taking away grace, of twisting something good so it is no longer as good as it should be. What some translations of Scripture call a "sin nature" is this partial corruption of the good that is human nature - it is not a creation properly speaking. We know evil is not a created thing because only God can create out of nothing, and He did not create evil. No one else has the power to create out of nothing; thus, evil is not a *something*, rather, it is a lack of something, a hole, a distortion of the good. We, puny humans that we are, only have the power to mar that which God has created. This marring, this taking away, this is evil. When evil is done intentionally, it is sin. A sinner is someone who is knowingly responsible for the evil he has committed. Marring God's creation is always evil, though it is not always sin, because it is possible to mar the good without intending it, without being personally responsible for the terrible consequences.

We have answered many questions, but we have left one question unanswered. We now see the effects of the Fall. We can understand more clearly why Adam and Eve did not have children before the Fall: that gift was to be given when full, intimate communion with God had been reached. But, why did Adam and Eve have children at all? The outlines of a possible answer to this question can now also be seen.

After we committed the great evil of the Fall, God did something we did not deserve. He turned to the serpent and told Satan not only that he had failed, but He told him something more, something incredible : "I will put enmity between you and the woman, between your seed and her seed" (Genesis 3:15).

Satan must have been absolutely shocked at this statement. True, as an angel, he knew the response that would come to him as a result of his actions. But, fortunately, though Satan knows the consequences of his own actions, he is finite. He cannot predict how God will respond to the actions of others.[*]

Satan knew what the first couple would lose if he led them astray. Had he not just successfully convinced Adam and Eve to throw away grace? Adam and Eve had chosen to sin. That is, they had given away their chance to have children. How could they live out the life of the Trinity in their own bodies if they didn't have

---

[*] This is the one thing an angel can learn, but only God can teach him.

the life of the Trinity left in their own souls? They were not in communion with God! They had treated each other like objects! If they were no longer in full communion with God, how could they be in communion with each other? How could God permit them the power to remain in any communion at all, much less permit them the *complete* interpenetration of persons that is pregnancy? What absurdity!

Rather, what a gift! For it was a total, free, unmerited gift from God to man. Even though Adam and Eve no longer merited the gift of being able to fully live out the life of the Trinity in their own bodies, God still permitted Eve to conceive and bear children. True, the pain of childbearing would be increased far beyond what would have been the case had we been obedient. Now Adam and his sons would have to struggle to provide for their families. Now, living out the life of the Trinity in our own bodies would necessarily include living out the Cross in our own bodies. Still, fallen man would be permitted to carry this great sign, the physical echo of the divine interpenetration of persons, so that the greatest gift of all could be accomplished, and Satan's lies about God's trustworthiness be overthrown.

God intended to give Himself to man despite the Fall.

Questions for discussion:

1) Compare and contrast what you knew about the Fall before reading this chapter and afterwards. What has changed?

2) "Clothes make the man." Discuss this statement in the context of the Fall.

3) Compare and contrast how you understood Faith, Hope and Love prior to reading this book and now. What has changed?

4) Some Christians assert the command to be fruitful and multiply is only a blessing, not a command. Discuss the merits of this assertion.

5) Discuss the concept of death as a kind of divorce in the context of the Christian understanding of marriage.

Scriptures for Contemplation

Gen 3:1-19 - Temptation, Fall, Consequences

Sirach 15:14-20 - Description of the Fall

Rom 2:19 - War between intellect and will

Catechism of the Catholic Church

Read and consider articles #385-421

IV. The Incarnation

> We find ourselves at the very heart of the Paschal
> Mystery, which completely reveals the spousal
> love of God. Christ is the Bridegroom because
> 'he has given himself': his body has been 'given,'
> his blood has been 'poured out.'…
>
> John Paul II
> *On the Dignity of Women*, #26

What God intends cannot be destroyed by something as puny as human error. An infinite chasm yawns between the one divine nature and human nature, yet God intended the two natures to somehow be joined. So, He began to work. He prepared the ground by choosing a people to be His Bride, and sending them prophet after prophet to speak of impending marriage. Now mankind was lost in a sea of sin, unable to turn towards God, but He continued to call, to protect, to prepare His People. Time after time, they fell. Time after time, He lifted them up and helped them towards the altar.

Finally, in the fullness of time, the Person of the Holy Spirit chose a woman, a daughter of His People, His Bride. In the moment of her conception, He prepared her with the same fullness of grace with which He had created Adam and Eve. Then He asked her the question he had prepared for Adam and Eve, "Will you marry yourself to me? Will you trust me, hope in me, love me as your Beloved?" They had said no. Mary whispered, "Yes."

In that instant, at the moment of her consent, God stretched Himself across that infinite chasm between the divine and human natures, leaping across the yawning deep and entering her womb, taking her ovum, wrapping it around Himself and making it fertile as He entered.

The Son totally possessed the divine nature. In that instant, He made a bridge of His own Person. In His Person, He took on human nature. Through His Person, He united human nature to the divine nature He already possessed. In the Person of the Son of God, the divine intellect and divine will united Himself to human flesh and a human soul, that is, a human intellect and a human will. In taking on human nature, the Son of God also took on the titles Jesus, which means "God Saves," and Christ, which means "The Anointed One."

In the Person of the Son, the divine nature and human nature married. The two natures are not intermingled or confused. Rather, the human intellect works in perfect harmony with the divine intellect. The human will works in perfect conformity with the divine will. Christ is not a human person, He is the Divine Person, the Son, God Himself, but living human nature, body and soul, to its full capacity.

Though always retaining the divine nature, the Son of God emptied Himself. He joined human nature to Himself and thereby sanctified it. The most glorious marriage mankind has ever known had begun. The consequences of this marriage continue to transform the world even as you read this.

The blood of Jesus Christ is infinitely holy, so holy that the smallest drop of His shed blood is sufficient to redeem all the sins of humanity, past, present and future. Now, we know this is true, but it raises a question we don't often ask. If the smallest drop is sufficient to redeem all of humanity's sins then why, at the first scourge of the whip, when that first drop of blood fell to the pavement in front of Pontius Pilate, why didn't Jesus begin a victory dance, singing, "I win, Satan loses, I am the King, there's the blood that redeems it all!" He could have done this. He didn't. Why didn't He?

He didn't do this because this is not how God lives His life. Remember, when God loves, He pours Himself out completely, He holds nothing back. Blood is the source of life (Leviticus 17:11). Though that first scourge, indeed, even the circumcision of Jesus, was enough to do the job of salvation, God still had more life, more love, more blood to give. So He did.

He accepted thirty-eight more lashes on His back, until it was a bloody mess. He accepted the crown of thorns, and blood streamed down His face and matted His hair. He carried that splintered wood on His shoulder uphill for a mile, breaking open both knees until blood streamed down to mark the path He walked. Because He still had more life, more love to give, He allowed nails to tear through His flesh. He hung for three hours as more blood soaked the wood of the cross, the splintered wood lacerating His back, turning the ground beneath into a sponge of blood. Even after He died, He had more blood to give, so He allowed a soldier to pierce His side with a lance, and still more blood and water flowed out. This is how God loves – with everything He is, holding nothing back. This is why we call it the Passion of the Christ, the Love of the Christ.

Why did He do this? He did it because this is how God loves. He did it to show us how much He loves us. He did it to take away our sins. He did it to model holiness to us, showing us how *we* are supposed to live. But He did it for another reason as well. He intends for us to be in intimate communion with Him. He intends us to be part of His family. This is why John the Baptist calls Jesus the Bridegroom (John 3:29). God marries us through His Son, Jesus

Christ. In this marriage, we not only have our own inheritance restored to us, we actually gain the very inheritance God the Father gives to God the Son.

Just as you or I cannot adopt our dog or marry our cat, so He cannot adopt us or marry us into His family as we are. We must be changed. Through the grace of the sacraments, we are empowered to participate in the intimate communion that God the Son has with God the Father and God the Holy Spirit. We are made sharers in the divine nature. St. Thomas Aquinas said it best, "The only-begotten Son of God, wanting to make us sharers in his divinity, assumed our nature, so that he, made man, might make men gods." (*Catechism of the Catholic Church*, #460, 2 Peter 1:4).

How can this be? St. John Damascene brought forward the example of a poker in a fire. If an iron poker is thrust into a hot fire, though it never itself becomes fire, still it begins to glow red-hot, white-hot, with the characteristics of fire. It gives off light and heat. It shares in the nature of the fire. Our God is a consuming fire (Hebrews 12:29). When the Son united human nature to Himself in the Incarnation, He plunged human nature into the consuming fire of God. This immersion in divinity was made complete in the Ascension, when He carried human nature into heaven and plunged it into the very heart of the Trinity's inner life.

The great chasm between human nature and divine nature remains, but because we are joined to the Body of Christ, we can access the divine nature through the Person of the Son of God. He is the *Pontifex*. He is the Bridge. He accomplished the marriage of human nature with divinity. Without Jesus, this sharing in the divine nature would be impossible. But He is God, and with God, all things are possible.

Questions for discussion:

1) How many intellects does Christ possess? How many wills? (see CCC #475) Does this surprise you? Why or why not?

2) Both John Paul II and Benedict XVI have remarked that the Marian aspect of the Church precedes the Petrine. How does this chapter explain that comment?

3) Consider Paul's use of two complementary metaphors in his writings - that of the Bride and Bridegroom, and that of the Head and the Body - in light of your previous answer. Does one of these metaphors precede or depend upon the other?

4) Compare the union of soul and body in the human nature possessed by man to the union of divine and human natures possessed by the one Person, Jesus Christ. How are these two alike? How are they different?

Scriptures for Contemplation

Isaiah 62:4-5 and Song of Songs 4:7-5:1 - Bride imagery

John 3:22-30 - Jesus is called the Bridegroom

Ephesians 5:21-33 and Revelation 19:7-8 - Marriage

Catechism of the Catholic Church
Read and consider articles #456-483.

V. The Problem of Pain

> Man suffers whenever he experiences any kind of evil…
> Man suffers on account of evil, which is a certain lack,
> limitation or distortion of good. We could say that
> man suffers because of a good in which he does not
> share, from which in a certain sense he is cut off, or of
> which he has deprived himself. He particularly suffers
> when he ought — in the normal order of things — to
> have a share in this good and does not have it. Thus, in
> the Christian view, the reality of suffering is explained
> through evil, which always, in some way, refers to a good.
>
> John Paul II
> *Salvifici Doloris*, #7

Upon seeing Christ's suffering and Cross, many people recoil. "What kind of God would want that kind of pain inflicted on someone?" they ask. Conversely, Christians sometimes look at the cross and conclude that pain must be good. After all, Jesus suffered and died for us. Jesus would never do an evil thing. Thus, pain must be a good thing. The conclusion seems obvious. But both ways of looking at the Cross misunderstand what has happened.

Pain is morally neutral, neither good nor bad in itself. But, at the same time, pain is a natural evil. What does that mean? How can both be true at the same time?

To understand this, we must recall the differences between grace, evil and sin. Grace is the power that keeps everything working harmoniously, without distortion. Evil is not a created thing, rather, it is a distortion of the good. When someone intentionally distorts the good, that person has committed a moral wrong, a sin. Even when the good is unintentionally distorted, even though it is not sin, the good is still marred.

So, to distinguish between evil and sin, we could say that sin describes how weak I become when I refuse to allow the full power of grace to enter the world. Evil describes how weak the world becomes when the full power of grace does not reside in it.

God created everything good. He created the universe to be at the service of man. Through the Fall, we stripped the world of much of its grace, leaving it unable to fulfill its function. It serves us to some extent, it is not totally corrupt, but it does not serve us as well as it did. This lack in nature is natural evil. The marvelous movie *The Princess Bride*, witnesses to the effects of the Fall when the masked man points out, "Life *is* pain, Princess. Anyone who tells you differently is selling something." Pain, at least to the extent it is present today, is not part of God's original design.

But the problem is larger than this. Not only is grace the power that keeps the world running harmoniously, grace is also our responsibility. God established mankind to be the steward who cares for the world. In Adam and Eve, He delegated part of His authority to us. God sends grace into the world. We are supposed to direct this grace, this power so as to help all creation bring greater glory to God.

So, man has two choices. He can accept that grace God sends new every morning, or he can reject it. If mankind rejects grace, then the world does not have the power needed to work harmoniously. We are all acquainted with machinery that breaks when it is run with insufficient power. The world is exactly that kind of machine. When we choose to reject the power of grace, the world inevitably fractures. Pain, a natural evil, is one of those fractures.

Now, we can reject grace in two ways. I can reject the grace God intends for me, and I can reject the grace God intends for the world around me. But, since I am part of the world around me, when I reject my own portion of grace I am simultaneously rejecting grace for the larger world as well.

There is some comforting news in all of this. While I can affect my own state of grace and I can affect the ability of natural objects to serve mankind well, I cannot directly harm your state of grace. I cannot strip grace directly from you, nor can you strip grace directly from me. Conversely, I cannot add grace to you, nor can you add grace to me. But I can affect the world around you. I can strengthen or weaken your support network.

So how does a natural good or evil affect us? When created things work the way they are supposed to, we find it easier to act in a morally good way. That is, when we are receiving grace from the world, we more easily recognize the empowering grace of God's generosity and we, as stewards, are much more likely enliven the world around us with grace. But, when the things of the world don't work well, we tend to become miserly, we tend to want others to suffer with us. Eve gave the apple to Adam; we pass our pain on as well. We can be stewards of grace present or stewards of grace lacking, but we are always stewards, for God has appointed us so.

If Eve had refused the apple from the serpent, if Eve had refused to give the apple to Adam, she would have graced the situation, that is, she would have invited grace into the situation and allowed it to do its work in the world. But, she didn't, in part because her support network had been weakened. Adam had failed to protect her from the serpent, he had stripped the world of power. The world no longer fully supported her. She saw that the world was no longer quite as generous; she knew this lack came from her love's failure to protect her.

Seeing him fail in his stewardship, she withdrew her generosity as well. Instead of protecting Adam from temptation, she thrust it at him. Now he was faced with the situation he had allowed her to experience, but on a much more intimate level. She had been directly tempted by a serpent. He was directly tempted by his greatest natural love. We know the results.

When I misuse the grace within me, I am now emptied of it. Grace is power precisely because it is the presence of God, and God will not abide in one who mars His work, He will not remain with one who does evil.

But because He made us the world's stewards, God will not heal the world without human assistance either. He gave us a share in His power and He will not revoke that gift. We must invite Him in.

How we respond to the natural goods and evils we meet every day influences how we decide to cooperate with the grace that dwells within us. The idea is this: no matter what comes our way, we will choose to cooperate with the power of grace within us, we will not choose to empty ourselves of it in despair or in retribution.

When we take a natural thing that is good and grace-filled – the human act of sex, for instance – and intentionally empty it of grace, through fornication or adultery, for example, we simultaneously empty ourselves of grace. But God sends grace new every morning. If we take the steps necessary to invite God back both into ourselves and into the situation we have emptied of grace, we can heal the damage we have done. It would be better had we never invited Him out. Yet, if we have, the damage can be repaired. But the damage will cause many to suffer while it exists.

God is the source of grace. We suffer because the world is short on grace. If grace is the road to heaven, pain is one of the potholes, that is, it is a possible impediment to reaching our destination if we hit it with the wrong attitude and/or misuse it.

However, if at the moment we encounter pain, we remain open to the God Who is the Source of grace, we become a pipeline. If we cooperate with the grace He places within us, He can use us as instruments to fill the empty spaces, the potholes in the road so to speak. The world's pain is lessened. Not only do we find ourselves on the road to heaven, but we have also helped make the road smoother for others to follow.

This is why St. Paul says "I chastise my body and bring it into subjection: lest perhaps, when I have preached to others, I myself should become a castaway" (1 Corinthians 9:27). He recognizes that the fallen world is too weak to be a reliable support. His own body, his own intellect, his own will, each being part of the fallen world, may thrust the apple into his face at any moment. So, in order to properly react in any situation, he must train himself to instantly recognize and rely on those graces that *are* present, wherever they may be. He must train himself to ignore the areas of creation that are marred and lean on the parts that are empowered by grace.

Suffering is always with us. The greatest saints invite physical suffering into their own lives not because suffering is good, but because suffering must be beaten, it must be overcome without an instant of hesitation, without an instant of regret. Like an athlete training for a marathon, a Christian who learns to do the good regardless of the amount of suffering poured upon his head has become again the steward of grace God intended him to be. He learns to work with God as God goes about healing the world. This is the sense in which Paul says, "I rejoice in my sufferings for your sake, and in my flesh I complete what is lacking in Christ's sufferings for the sake of His Body, the Church" (Col 1:24).

Pain is a warning that grace is missing. When I begin to suffer, I am supposed to recognize that the situation I have entered is short of grace. God has given to us the responsibility to help the world give Him glory. It can't do that if it is short on grace. Someone has to heal this breech.

As long as I willingly join myself to Christ's cross during each awful experience of suffering, God will use my presence to pour His own powerful grace back into each situation and heal it. He will use me as the conduit to enter into the wounded world.

The suffering I feel is not good – it is a sign that I have encountered evil, a distortion of good, a lack of good. But my presence in that situation, my willingness to help heal it, *that* is good. I cannot be there without suffering, but I *must* be there to be the instrument through which this part of the world is healed. So I must accept the suffering in order to accomplish the healing that God intends for the world.

Everyone knows pain is evil, but most do not realize pain is also very important work. Instead, many people see only the pain of the Cross and mistakenly think Christians view pain as good. They see only the pain, and cannot see beyond it to the grace. Thus, they do not understand why one man chose to dwell in the center of our desert of pain. One man stood tall in the thrashing, fractured world, stood still and absorbed into Himself all the pain the world could deal out. He did this so that the grace, the power necessary to heal the world, could pour out through Him like water through a pipe, like water to a dry desert, to heal a dying world.

Questions for discussion:

1) Some say the bodily mortifications the saints subjected themselves to show that these saints had a distorted understanding of the body. What reply would you make to this?

2) Give examples of people today who voluntarily accept physical suffering in pursuit of some goal. How do their sufferings, and their reasons for accepting it, compare with the sufferings and goals of the greatest saints?

3) How is the interaction between Adam and Eve in the Garden similar to and/or different from the interaction between each person's soul and body in this world?

4) As we grow in holiness, will we suffer greater or fewer temptations? Why?

5) Pope John Paul II never mentions pain or suffering in any of his "Theology of the Body" Wednesday audiences. Instead, he wrote an entire encyclical on the subject. Why?

Scriptures for Contemplation

Col 1:24-29 – Making up in my body what is lacking in Christ.

Gal 6:1-6 – Bear one another's burdens, fulfill the law of Christ

Eph 3:7-13 – I suffer for your glory

Phil 1:7-30 – Suffering advances the Gospel

Mt 27:32 – Simon of Cyrene

Catechism of the Catholic Church

Read and consider articles #164, 385, 1502-1505, 1521

VI. The Sacraments

> The Eucharist is the Sacrament of our Redemption. It is the Sacrament of the Bridegroom and the Bride... Christ is united with this 'body' as the bridegroom with the bride... Since Christ, in instituting the Eucharist, linked it in such an explicit way to the priestly service of the Apostles, it is legitimate to conclude that he thereby wished to express the relationship between man and woman."
>
> John Paul II
> *On the Dignity of Women*, #26

From our point of view, the most important title God carries is that of Bridegroom. When we begin to consider this title in all its richness, several things begin to appear before us. The Latin word for sacrament is derived from *sacramentum* which means "oath," but the Greek word for sacrament is *mysterion*, or "mystery."

Of all the seven sacraments, only one sacrament is called a sacrament (*mysterion*) in Scripture: "this is a great mystery, but I speak of Christ and His Church" (Ephesians 5:32). Though the Eucharist lies at the heart of our relationship to Christ, it does so precisely because matrimony is the form of our union with Christ. When we understand that marriage forms the sacraments like our souls form our bodies, we begin to see that each of the seven sacraments Jesus established empower an aspect of our marriage to God. This is why marriage both begins and ends Scripture, and why it is the single constant theme of Scripture (Gen 2:23 and Rev 22:17). Marriage is the primordial sacrament.

When a dispute arose between the disciples of John the Baptist about Jesus, it occurred in the context of baptism (John 3:22-30). It was during this dispute that Jesus was first called the Bridegroom.

Through the use of this title, John explicitly described baptism as a marriage rite. In fact, baptism is like the marriage vow; it is the sacrament that makes each one of us a newlywed to Jesus, the Bridegroom. Through this sacrament, we not only receive the inheritance of grace lost through Adam and Eve, we gain that which they never fully had – participation in the divine nature. True, as a result of the collapse of our nature after the removal of grace, we still have a tendency to want to collapse again into sin by again removing the grace that God has given us. The "creases" that result from the Fall, like the creases in a collapsible water jug, are not easily overcome. This weakness in our nature, the tendency to sin, is called "concupiscence." Still, if we rely on God's grace, these weaknesses can be overcome. If we rely on the grace of God and lean on the strength of our Bridegroom, we can avoid sin and "Be holy as God is holy" (Matthew 5:48).

Indeed, the grace of God will ultimately restore all the failed harmonies of our human state prior to our original fall from grace. Through the Bridegroom, mankind already has had control over creation restored, for now a man, a priest, can affect the very substance of bread and wine so that they are no longer present, but rather the glorified Christ is. In the reception of the sacraments, we already begin to share in the divine nature.

Because of this, man and woman, if they lean into the grace of the sacraments, especially the sacrament of marriage, can give self to another totally, without abusing one another. As we learn more about the Divine Bridegroom (Jesus), His Bride (the Church), and how to live His life, God sends grace to us to strengthen and clarify our intellects and wills. We become more aware of grace. Our intellects and wills become sharper and more powerful, they work together more harmoniously, and we are more easily able to avoid sin. Finally, our soul and body will be indissolubly reunited at the resurrection of the dead. All of this work is begun in baptism. It lays the foundation that every newlywed couple needs to survive.

But, as any married couple knows, the relationship between newlyweds needs to mature and strengthen. We cannot live as newlyweds our whole lives, nor should we. Still, we do not have the power to alter our relationship with God – only God's grace can give us the power to mature in the way we need to mature. Therefore, He gives us confirmation, which is the power to mature and strengthen our relationship with Him. Confirmation is an obligation assumed at the moment of baptism (CCC 1306, canons 889.1 and 890). It is a choice only in the sense that we each have a choice to live God's life or to reject His life. Through confirmation, we gain the power to live out our marriage to Jesus in a fully mature fashion.

Eucharist is the Body, Blood, Soul and Divinity of the risen Christ, it is the flesh of God. We, the Bride of Christ, celebrate the Nuptial Feast of the Mass in order to partake of His flesh. Thus, it is perfectly correct to say that, at the Wedding Feast, the flesh of the Bridegroom enters the flesh of the Bride. In Eucharist, God consummates His marriage to us. It is the only sacrament that fully signifies heaven (Revelation 19:9). Indeed, the whole point of heaven is to partake of the intimate communion that is Eucharist.

How is the Wedding Feast prepared? When we have guests over for a celebration, it is the family, the parents and children, who prepare the feast for the guests. In the same way, Holy Orders is the Father making His Son present to prepare the marriage feast for the Bride. At the moment of consecration, the priest *is*, in a certain sense, Jesus. He *is* the Bridegroom. The priest is not, at that moment, merely a symbol or representative. In a certain sense, he *is* Jesus. This is why men alone are consecrated priests. Just as woman, in sex and pregnancy, lives out the communion and interpenetration of Persons in the Trinity more perfectly than ever man can, so man, in Holy Orders, lives Christ the Bridegroom more perfectly than ever woman can. Man and woman together image God in their bodies, but woman is permitted to live out the divine image in her own body more fully. Man and woman are, by baptism, made priests of the Most High, but certain men are permitted to live that divine priesthood out in their lives more fully. Woman images God through the sacred nature of her body; man images Him through the supernatural gift of the sacrament.

When we have committed adultery against the Bridegroom by loving someone or something more than our Spouse, only repentance and Reconciliation allows us to renew our wedding vows. In this sacrament, we join with Him in condemning our own adultery, we reaffirm our love for Him alone and above all else. With our own mouths and in our own bodies we live out a foretaste of the Last Judgement, when we must stand in union with our Spouse and condemn all of the attacks upon Him, especially our own.

Finally, Anointing of the Sick is how the Bridegroom heals the Bride when she is ill, and how He prepares her for the journey to His Father's house when the honeymoon on earth is over.

Marriage is the primordial sacrament precisely because it is the form of all the sacraments. "Matrimony [is] directed towards the salvation of others; if [it] contribute[s] as well to personal salvation, it is through service to others that [it does] so." (*Catechism of the Catholic Church*, #1534). The purpose of marriage is salvation: not salvation for me, but salvation for the person whom I marry. In this sense, each spouse is servant to the other. Each spouse is Christ to the other. This is why St. Paul tells us to "be subject to one another out of reverence for Christ" (Ephesians 5:21), and follows by saying "Wives, be subject to your husbands, as to the Lord." He wants both husbands and wives to remember that matrimony is not directed towards my salvation, it is directed towards the salvation of my spouse. He wants us to remember that this salvation finds its foundation in the relationship between the Bridegroom and the Bride. The vow I make in marriage to my spouse is the freely chosen vow of serving her for the rest of her life, so that she may reach salvation.

This is, perhaps, best explained through an example. In the marvelous Italian movie, *Life is Beautiful*, the main character is training to be a waiter. In order to be a good waiter, he needs to know how to bow, but he does not do it very well. His uncle, the head waiter, gently corrects him, "Think of sunflowers. They bow to the sun. But if you see some that are too bowed down, that means they are dead. You are serving, you are not a servant. Serving is a supreme art. God is the first servant. God serves man but He is not a servant to men."

Love is not servitude. Love is the decision, the choice to serve. True, servitude sometimes begins with a choice: indentured servants were at one time quite common. Enslavement, on the other hand, is not a choice at all, it is the taking away of freedom. Love is neither servitude nor enslavement.

Love is the freely-entered, continuing choice to give another person everything I am: all my talents, my skills, my hopes, my fears, my dreams - all of it. For a man, it means every talent, every skill, every hope is directed towards assisting his spouse, helping her become even more glorious than she already is. It is indeed a kind of artistry, for the artist gives himself to the canvas in a very similar way, and for very similar purposes - to make the canvas and the paints much, much more glorious than they are.

The difference, of course, is that love is directed towards a person, towards helping *this woman* achieve full glory. It isn't just a bunch of paint or a canvas upon which I can impose my own vision. Rather, this person has a reason for existing - God made her with a purpose in mind. My love for her is the decision to act with God as a co-creator, as an assistant to the Master, so that she may reach the full glory God intended for her. I don't impose my vision on her, rather I help her reach God's vision for her, help her reach her divinely-ordained perfection. By doing this, I become part of divine perfection as well. I am perfected as she is perfected, she by being served, I by serving. Together, we become like unto God. This is what it means to say that human persons can share in the divine nature. God is love.

This view of the sacraments is helpful, but it raises a question. We know that every sacrament imparts power. Why do so few people who have received sacraments seem to possess the mature power the grace imparts?

Even as we accept the power of a sacrament the work of grace is not yet completed in us. Having power is not the same as knowing how to use power. We can each think of numerous instances when we have known someone who clearly has a specific physical, mental or social power but uses the power inappropriately or not at all. So it is with grace. When we consider Adam and Eve, when we consider how God has inscribed Himself both upon our very bodies and upon the communion of persons that our bodies make possible, we realize that we must allow that same grace to teach us how to live out in our bodies the power God has given. Having the power is not enough. We have to learn how to use it. We learn this by service. So far, we have discussed the service man owes to woman and woman owes to man. But there is another aspect of service that is just as important. In fact, it is impossible to understand the Church unless we understand this second aspect.

> The church cannot therefore be understood as the… universal sacrament of salvation unless we keep in mind the great mystery involved in the creation of man as male and female and the vocation of both to conjugal love, to fatherhood and to motherhood.
>
> John Paul II
> *Letter to Families, #19*

Conjugal love, fatherhood, motherhood: in a certain sense, the Church can only be understood by understanding the married vocation to have sex and have children. The vocation to fatherhood and motherhood, the vocation to be a Christian, is intimately bound up with sex, the transmission of life, and love, the service of life. Both physically and spiritually, being a parent is about living a life of service to our spouse and our children.

John Paul II gives us the key. We must view the sacrament(s) in the perspective of marriage, fatherhood, motherhood, the transmission of life and the service to life. Every sacrament helps us live out some aspect of unitive, one-body love, that is, each sacrament helps us live our marriage to the Bridegroom, Jesus Christ. Once we see this, we can also see another remarkable thing. Recall the hierarchy that God established from the beginning of creation: God has headship over mankind. He created man to have headship over woman. Man and woman would together help creation grow towards God.

As was mentioned before, God's plans cannot be derailed by something as puny as human error. Consider the hierarchy established in Jesus Christ: the God-Man's authority is drawn from God the Father. Christ, in turn, cares for and has headship over His Bride, the Church. Together, the Bridegroom and the Bride have total control over creation, for through the power of His grace and the power of the liturgy given to His Bride, man's words can transform reality. When we pour water and invoke the Triune Name, human beings are transformed into very children of God. When the priest says, "This is my Body", the substance of bread and wine depart and the substance of the Bridegroom abides. When the words of absolution pour forth from the priest's mouth, the wind of Christ's breath blows our sins as far as east is from west, transforming us into purity. When man and woman unite in sex, when sperm and egg begin to unite in her body, God immediately creates and infuses an immortal human soul. God gives us natural and supernatural control over creation.

In Christ, God did not just re-establish the original order of creation given to us in Adam and Eve. We have more power now than Adam and Eve ever had in the Garden. The original hierarchy of creation described in the second meditation is not lost. It is elevated beyond our wildest dreams.

Adam could not make his children partakers of the divine nature by washing them with water. Adam could not confect the Eucharist. Through the power of the Bridegroom, Jesus Christ, the power He and the Bride together wield over creation, creation now serves mankind in a manner infinitely superior to anything that was possible prior to the Fall. This is why the Easter Vigil liturgy speaks of the Fall with the words, "O happy fault, O necessary sin of Adam, which gained for us so great a Redeemer!"

Questions for discussion:
1) Compare and contrast what you knew about the sacraments before reading this and after. What has changed?
2) Why is marriage the only sacrament not conferred by a priest?
3) Compare and contrast the view of marriage presented here with the view of marriage given to us by the larger culture.
4) Why does the Church insist "God's plans never fail"?

Scriptures for Contemplation

2 Macc 7:22 and Psalm 139:13-14 - The Mystery of Creation

John 2:1-11 - Washing at the Wedding Feast

Matt 22:1-9, Rev 19:5-9, Rev 22:17 - God's Wedding Feast

Catechism of the Catholic Church

Read and consider articles #770-776.

VII.　Married Life

> The great mystery, which is the church and humanity
> in Christ, does not exist apart from the great mystery
> expressed in the 'one flesh,' that is, in the reality of marriage
> and the family.... Unfortunately, Western thought...
> has been gradually moving away from this teaching.
>
> John Paul II
> *Letter to Families, #19*

Hopefully, it is now clear why these two sentences sum up both what the theology of the body is about and why it is being brought forward at this time in human history with such great emphasis. The teachings present in this understanding of God and man are not new to Christianity, but they are vibrantly new to this generation of Christians.

Sadly, since much of Christian education and most Western philosophy has been slowly degenerating since the Enlightenment, very few modern Christians understand Christianity. The Baltimore Catechism was a great tool for children. We are adults. Ten-year-old children cannot be given the fullness of the Faith because they aren't old enough to understand it. Indeed, as was noted before, the Theology of the Body is something young children cannot really fully grasp. Yet, these same young persons must be intimately familiar with the Theology of the Body by the time they reach maturity, for it is not right that any adult Catholic be ignorant of how God saves us.

Many Christians view sex as something dirty. Oddly, they think this way for good reason. The Jews know that touching the Torah, the sacred scrolls of Scripture, defiles the hands. Why does touching the holy defile us? Because we are defiled before we even begin to approach the holy. As we approach purity, we become aware of our own impurity, and our own need to be washed clean. Like a child called back home at twilight, we become aware of our soiled hands and clothes only as we approach the light radiating from our home. Holiness defiles us in the sense that holiness makes us aware of our own preexisting defilement. Though the idea that sex is dirty mistakenly attributes our sins to God's great gift, it still shows a dim understanding of the enormous holiness that sex is.

> Conjugal love goes to Christ the Bridegroom through a human union...
> John Paul II
> *General Audience, 23 Nov 1994*

We already know that the Church not only cannot be understood except through the mystery of conjugal love, but that she does not exist apart from marriage and family. The Bridegroom revealed God through His own Body. The sacrifice and total gift He made of His Flesh established His Body, the Church. Make no mistake: we cannot understand God unless we understand the most intimate of human relationships. The universal sacrament which is the Church cannot be understood without understanding conjugal love. Conjugal love cannot be understood apart from the human union.

When we consider the total outpouring of Jesus' blood at the Crucifixion, every drop poured out for us, we must also recognize that the ancients considered bodily fluids, like semen, a kind of blood. This is not a coincidence. We gain life through His total gift of Himself to us. We gain life through the total gift of Bridegroom to Bride.

The Eucharist is the Body, Blood, Soul and Divinity of Jesus Christ. In His glorified Body, the Eucharist is God giving Himself totally to man. Whether we call it Cross or Eucharist, this is the single Paschal Mystery. The Passion, Death, Resurrection and Ascension of Christ, the whole of the Paschal Mystery, is accomplished in the flesh. An adult who meditates on this reality touches on the heart of the Christian mystery.

There is an infinite distance between human nature and divine nature. Because of the effects of original sin, there is also, in a certain sense, an infinite gap between myself and the person I intend to marry.

Christ bridged the infinite gap between human and divine nature by joining the divine nature to human nature in His own Person. Because of Christ, I can bridge the divine-human gap as well, for baptism joins me to the Body of Christ. I am married to the Person of Christ through my baptism. But my intended is likewise married to the Person of Christ through her baptism. Christ bridges two infinite chasms at once. In marriage, the Person of Christ bridges the infinite chasm between myself and my intended in an absolutely intimate way. Through the sacrament of marriage, man and woman are joined together in Jesus' Person just as divine and human nature are.

This has startling implications. I can share in the divine nature only because Christ is the Bridge. Similarly, I can interact with my spouse at the height, which is conjugal love, only *through* Christ. Because of marriage, I do not simply have a relationship with Christ in my intellect; I have a relationship with Christ through the living, breathing body-soul unity who is my spouse. I live out my relationship with my Bridegroom through my relationship with another human person. How I treat my spouse is exactly how I treat Christ, because I can only touch my spouse through His Person.

When we understand this, we understand why the Mass is called the Nuptial Feast. Marriage between two human persons is the training ground in which each spouse learns how to live married life with Christ. Eucharist is the divine marriage bed. When we receive Eucharist, we begin to realize that what married couples do in the marriage bed is meant to provide a pale, physical image of the splendid, total communion, the total outpouring of self to another, the interpenetration of the divine persons we have referred to again and again.

But what is true in one direction is also true in the other. Thus, when I turn to my spouse in the marital act, I am living out my relationship to Jesus in the Eucharist. God gives Himself entirely to me in the Eucharist. He calls me to give myself entirely back to Him. God creates each human person, and then pours Himself out completely to each human person through the blood of the Cross, establishing the fullness of life within each of us.

How the man gives of himself in the marital act is meant to image how Christ gave of Himself on the Cross. How the woman receives the man in the marital act is meant to image how all mankind receives the blood of Christ poured out for us, His Bride. The result of this communion of divine Person with human persons can be the creation of an immortal image of the living God, the generation of a third human person. The consuming fire of the love between the Father and the Son breathes forth the Person of the Spirit; similarly, in the heat of sexual passion, the bodies of man and wife can breathe forth a third person, the person of their child. The marriage act at its height images the inner life of the Trinity, the divine life we are all meant to partake in. Sex between bridegroom and bride establishes on earth and in the very act, a living, sacred image of the divine family of God and His relationship to man.

The implications are incredible. We live out both the life of God and the entirety of salvation history in our own bodies through the sexual act.

Consider the correspondences: the three Persons of the Trinity interpenetrate one another, Father and Son together breathing forth the Spirit. In sex, man interpenetrates woman and, together with God, Who creates and infuses the human soul, a third immortal person comes into existence. Just as God is eternally fertile, so man is always fertile. Just as fallen man is not always open to grace, so woman is not always able to conceive new life. God gives fallen man life-giving grace, man receives it and new life springs forth within him. In sex, man pours himself out into the woman, the woman receives him and new life can spring forth in her from this gift. Through the pouring out of His life-giving grace, God divinizes man, bringing him to new life in Himself. In the divinely fruitful act, man lives out Godhead for a moment and woman lives it out for months. Through the interpenetration and pouring out of himself into woman, woman is, in a sense, "divinized," she is completely interpenetrated by another person, an immortal child. She feeds this child with her own flesh, her breasts, as Jesus feeds us with His flesh in Eucharist. When a pregnant woman receives Eucharist, three persons abide in communion within one body.

> ...reverence for Christ and respect which the author of Ephesians speaks of is none other than a spiritually mature form of that mutual attraction revealed for the first time in Genesis (Gn 2:23-25) ...[which is itself] none

other than the blossoming of the gift of fear - one of the seven gifts of the Holy Spirit (1 Thess 4:4-7)...

This seems to be the integral significance of the sacramental sign of marriage. In that sign, through the language of the body, man and woman encounter the great mystery. ...[In the] language of the practice of love, fidelity, and conjugal honesty... conjugal life becomes in a certain sense liturgical.

John Paul II
General Audience, 4 July 1984

On the anniversary of America's independence, the Holy Father explained how we live divine freedom. Together, man and woman live out the Godhead in their own bodies. They become a communion of persons whose life is love. Thus, conjugal love, including sexual communion between husband and wife, when it is a lived expression of love, fidelity, and conjugal honesty, becomes "liturgical."

What does it mean to say sex is "liturgical?" Liturgy is the participation of the people of God in the work of God. Indeed, the very words "liturgy" and "energy" both come from the same Greek word - *ergon* or "work." God's work is our salvation. Liturgy is how God applies the sanctifying work of the Cross to the whole of mankind. Liturgy sanctifies the world. Thus, when we say the full, true life-giving love embodied in marital sex is essentially liturgical, we are saying sex between spouses can help sanctify the world.

When it is an expression of the divine ethos, sex in marriage can help bring about the peace, joy and harmony of the Kingdom of Heaven on earth. In order for this to happen, however, the spouses must each totally give himself and herself to each other, not just as Adam and Eve did before the Fall, but as Christ did for the Church. Jesus poured out every drop of His blood for us. He gave Himself into creation and spilled out all the life He had within Him unto creation. God did not wear a condom when He created the universe. He wore nothing when He saved us. Instead, He hung naked on the Cross - nothing between Himself and us. It would be sacrilege to wrap the Eucharist in a condom before we receive Him. We are to receive all that He is. In the Eucharist, we delightfully open ourselves to Him so that He might ravish us. My spouse is Christ to me. How we act towards each other in our marriage bed, is how we act towards Christ in the Eucharist. We can touch our spouse because we first are His. He expects us to give ourselves entirely to Him, whether in sex with our spouse or at the Nuptial Feast.

The marvelous pleasure we feel in the marital act is an echo of the joy God takes in creation. God pours Himself out completely to us, and asks us to do the same to His image, our spouse. He gives Himself to us when we are open to His life and He gives Himself to us when we are not. When we as spouses put physical or chemical barriers between each other in the sexual act, we put barriers between ourselves and Jesus.

Contraception, whether through a device, surgery or chemistry, violates the image of God we are to live out in our bodies. Instead of living Jesus, we live out the message, "I don't *want* to be like you, God. I don't want to love. Or trust. Or share." We have already made that mistake once – that was the mistake that cost us our inheritance in the beginning. Through the power of God, we have regained our inheritance. Let us not be foolish and throw it away again.

Questions for discussion:
1) Re-read the quote that opens this chapter and explain why an attack on marriage is an attack on Christ Himself.
2) The Holy Father spoke of the mutual attraction of Genesis actually being rooted in fear of the Lord, one of the Spirit's seven gifts. Why is this true?
3) He goes on to say that sex is not the great mystery, rather, it is an encounter with the great mystery. Explain that remark.

Scriptures for Contemplation
Matthew 5:48 and 1 Peter 1:14-16 - Being as holy as God
Gen 38:9-10 - Onan's act of contraception
Gen 1:28 and Mark 10:13 - Blessings of God

Catechism of the Catholic Church
Read and consider articles #1643-1658

VIII. Celibacy

Joseph, in obedience to the Spirit, found in the Spirit the source of love, the conjugal love which he experienced as a man. And this love proved to be greater than this 'just man' could ever have expected within the limits of his human heart.

John Paul II
Guardian of the Redeemer, #19

In this way, Pope John Paul II begins to answer one of the central questions raised by the theology of the body. If God established "the creation of man as male and female and the vocation of both to conjugal love, to fatherhood and to motherhood," as the Pope indicates in his *Letter to Families,* then how can celibacy be a vocation? If the living out of the Godhead in our own bodies is so crucial to us, then why don't we beget children in heaven? In heaven, we are "neither married nor given in marriage" (Matthew 22:30), so it doesn't sound like much procreation is going on there. If procreation is so important to us, why does it stop?

Marriage and the generation of human persons is not necessary in heaven because in heaven we will be glorious witnesses to a much more perfect generation. Since we are part of the Body of Christ, we will be fully aware, in every fiber of our beings, of the processions of Divine Persons. The sacrament of marriage we live out here is thus a divine training ground for something much better.

Indeed, this is part of the reason we know Mary is Ever-Virgin. It is also why we know celibacy is the "higher way" to perfection. Now, O gentle reader, the previous statement merits strenuous objection: "How can *celibacy* be the higher way? Especially given all that has been written about conjugal love, marriage and sex here?

Marriage establishes the one-flesh union of persons, it generates immortal persons, it allows us to live out the very image of the inner life of God in our flesh! How can anyone say *celibacy is the higher way?*" The very thought sounds like a complete contradiction of all that has gone before.

It isn't. The reasons why this is so require some careful thought. We must begin by clearing away a misconception. Whenever celibacy is brought forward in discussion, the discussion will eventually turn towards the Holy Family. Mary is Ever-Virgin. Whether we speak of the time before, during or after the birth of the Son of God, her virginity remained intact. Joseph and Mary, though truly married, never had sexual relations. As a result, some people draw the conclusion that sex, though permitted in marriage, dirties or demeans the marriage relationship, that it is a necessary evil in marriage which God allows only because of our lust and hardness of hearts.*

This is not so. It is not the case that the Holy Family is holy *because* Mary and Joseph never had sex. Nor is it true that married people can only be holy, or will be holier, if they avoid sex - indeed, quite the opposite might often be the case.

People who don't have sex are not necessarily holier than spouses who do. Individual married couples can be and frequently are holier than many of the celibate people around them. When a sexually active married couple is holy, it is necessarily *because* their sex life is fully living out the life of God. The married couple is holy when their sexual relations are marvelously healthy and holy, as the previous meditation, "Married Life" described.

---

* Some will even point to St. Paul's first letter to the Corinthians to substantiate this view (1 Cor 7:1-7).

When God tells us that celibacy is the higher way, He does not mean to imply that marriage is an obstacle to holiness. Indeed, God established marriage as the means by which every person is to be made holy, though a means not all are called to use directly. Still, even celibates require marriage in order to attain holiness. Marriage presents to the whole world, to every living person, a concrete, in-the-flesh example of what it means to live out the intimate communion of persons in our own bodies.

> By matrimony, therefore, the souls of the contracting parties are joined and knit together more directly and more intimately than are their bodies, and that not by any passing affection of sense or spirit, but by a deliberate and firm act of the will; and from this union of souls by God's decree, a sacred and inviolable bond arises.
>
> Pope Pius XI
> *Chaste Marriage*, #7

As St. Paul reminds us, the mutual nourishment and cherishing each of the other in marriage is critical to understanding Christ's love for us (Eph 5: 25-32). This lived example of the communion of persons is absolutely necessary for celibate persons, for it is only through the lived example of married persons and the families they shepherd through the world that celibates gains a real understanding of the intimate life of love God calls them to when He calls them to Himself and the Trinitarian Family of Persons. Similarly, the life of the celibate person is absolutely indispensable to every married couple, for it is only through close contact with the life of the celibate that married persons fully understand the kind of intimacy God calls us to when He calls us to union with the Divine Persons.

Jesus will not have sex with us in heaven, nor will we have sex with each other. Rather, we won't need the sign, the symbol, which sex is. Instead, we will have the full intimate communion with the Divine Persons that every human person has always been called to. Pope Pius XI's words demonstrate why celibates must embrace and protect marriage as necessary to their own vocation while also demonstrating why married couples must embrace and protect the life of the celibate or risk losing their own ability to live their vocation to holiness.

The individual sexual state of each person, celibate or married, lives out an example. Fallen man absolutely requires both examples in order to fully understand his own relationship with God.

In the vows of marriage, the spouses are consecrated to act towards each other as they would towards Christ. Each person is consecrated to be Christ for the other. In the vows of celibacy, however, the celibate is consecrated directly to Christ Himself.

The difference is obvious. While my spouse may not always live up to Christ's standards, Christ always does. Thus, my spouse may, through human weakness, inadvertently make it more difficult for me to grow towards holiness, while Christ never does.

Thus, celibacy is a higher road to holiness in the sense that celibates encounter fewer obstacles to living a life totally devoted to God. Mary and Joseph are not holier primarily because they were celibate, rather, their celibacy is a consequence of the specific life God called them to lead, a consequence of their own quests for holiness, their own responses to God's grace. But how can this be true, given everything that has been written so far?

Celibacy is based in marriage. This might sound odd, but it is true. Scripture provides the links necessary to see this. We know from Scripture that man and wife can separate from their conjugal rights for a time in order to commune with God in prayer (1 Corinthians

7:5). Prayer is communion with God, but it is not the highest form of communion. We are put into the most intimate communion with God through the sacraments. Baptism, for instance, joins us intimately to Christ. I am intimately bound to, married to, Christ through my baptism. Similarly, my spouse is married to Christ through her baptism.

Think about this for a moment. Jesus Christ is not only the mediator between God and man, He is the mediator between myself and my spouse. I am bound to *my spouse* in sacramental marriage only because I am first married to *Him* through baptism.

I am married to Him. She is married to Him. We know the Person of the Son of God stretched Himself across the infinite chasm between the divine nature and the human nature, becoming the bridge that joined the two. In a similar way, Jesus is the bridge that joins me to my spouse. Because of our fallen human nature, there is, in a certain sense, an unbridgeable chasm between myself and the woman I intend to marry. The chasm is bridged in the Person of Christ. Thus, I can marry my wife and cleave to her only because each of us is first married to Him. In a very real sense, I am only in contact with my spouse because I am first in contact with Jesus through baptism. Whatever I do to my spouse, I do to Him first, for I can only reach her through Him. That is what the sacrament of marriage does - it creates this unbreakable communion of persons.

If the whole of my union with my spouse is maintained only through Jesus, then certainly my intimate physical union with my spouse is maintained through Him. In fact, the pleasure and joy I take in intimate physical union with my spouse is meant to mirror the pleasure and joy I take in my intimate spiritual union with Jesus.

In other words, I have sex with my wife in part to express the joy, both physical and spiritual, I take in Life, that is, in God. My spouse is Christ for me. My whole being, body and soul, needs to respond to the grace Christ gives me. In prayer and in the sacraments, I cry out joyfully in my union with Christ, my spouse. Sex images this. Sex is a pale shadow of the joy we will experience in our own flesh when we are in intimate communion God. This sexual union, when it results in procreation, brings forth a second aspect of service: consecration to serve the child that we, as spouses, have helped bring forth.

"This is all very nice," you might be thinking, "but it doesn't explain why Mary and Joseph were celibate, nor why anyone is called to celibacy." Remember that the Three Persons of the one God is the First Family. After the Last Judgment, we will live intimate, loving communion with God, the family of Persons whose life is love, in our own flesh, in our resurrected bodies. This is what we are made for: to live out in our bodies the inner family life of the Trinity, Who is the family of divine Persons, God.

Now, consider who Mary and Joseph were living with. As the parents to God in the flesh, Mary and Joseph already had the intimate physical reality of family communion with God. Mary is God's true mother, biological and spiritual, and Joseph, though not a biological father, is certainly a true father in the human sense to God. After all, Joseph gave Jesus life on the day he refused to have Mary stoned for suspected adultery. Subsequently, he was all that a true human father could be to his Son, except in biology.

Thus, in the three persons of the Holy Family, two human persons were in direct, intimate, loving, family communion with God in their own flesh. By their true fatherhood and true motherhood towards the child Jesus, each had already been consecrated by their marriage vows into direct service to Christ. For most married couples, the vows of marriage consecrate them to serve the children they procreate. For this particular married couple, the child they served was God Himself. Thus, their marriage vows were the only marriage vows ever taken that consecrated the spouses to celibacy. After all, their child was not only an image of Christ, He *was* Christ. And now we begin to glimpse the full glory of their marriage.

In their small hovel, they lived out the most complete foretaste of heaven anyone on earth has ever known. Mary and Joseph didn't need the shadow which sex provides - they had something much better. Even the best sex between human persons is an infinitely distant also-ran in comparison to the ecstasy of heaven. Mary and Joseph had family communion with God in their own flesh. Their intimacy with God was and is every parent's loving relationship with his child, an intimacy which only a parent can fully appreciate. This intimate family life, the life they lived with Jesus, with God, was their ecstasy. Sexual orgasm would have been a step down. Who looks for water when he has wine?

And herein is the explanation for celibacy, indeed, it is only in this way that celibacy is better than the sacrament of marriage. Celibacy is *only* better than marriage if I am living out in my own body this intimate family relationship with Jesus in the flesh.

How can I live an intimate relationship with Jesus in the flesh, given that He is now ascended? There is only one way. He gives us His flesh, His whole Person, in the Eucharist.

Celibacy only works if I have an intense in-the-flesh relationship with Christ in the Eucharist, Christ in the Flesh, either through physical reception or spiritual communion. And it is the realization of this fact that separates the consecrated celibate from the person who has not vowed to undertake celibate life. From the beginning, God said that it is not good for man to be alone (Gen 2:18). This has always been true and will always be true for every human person. We need in-flesh communion with another person. That is why we have bodies. Without in-flesh communion, we are incomplete, and we experience the constant, aching pain of being incomplete. This is the pain of those separated from their spouses by death, by divorce or by an inability to find the right person to marry.

By making an act of the will and consciously choosing to consecrate himself to celibacy, the consecrated celibate knows God's will for him and aligns himself to it. In contrast, the widow or widower did not intend the state they now occupy, nor does the person separated from his spouse, for no one marries in order to be separated from their spouse. Similarly, the single person who has not taken vows of celibacy or marriage has not yet been able to discern God's will - this is why he has not yet taken one vow or the other. In many of these cases, such persons have not consciously chosen what God wills for them, if only because they are still trying to discern what God's will is.

So, insofar as life's circumstances renders me unwillingly single, I know I am incomplete, that I do not have the in-flesh communion God intends for me, and I do not yet fully know how God intends my problem to be solved. Even if I am married, while I gain in-flesh communion through life with my spouse, the communion between us is marred by our own respective imperfections. But, if I am willingly celibate, if I willingly choose to devote myself to Christ in the Eucharist and strive constantly to grow in my relationship with Him, then I have the best possible life on this earth.

But this points to the heart of the problem. If I am unwillingly celibate and I do not have a relationship with God in the Flesh, then celibacy is not holier than marriage, rather, it is much, much worse than being married. Indeed, it is very nearly as close to hell on earth as anyone could devise. As a child of Adam, I am made to participate in a communion of persons in the flesh. If this communion is denied me, if I am not in a human communion of persons (married) or a divine communion of persons (Eucharistic relationship), I cannot live out the communion of persons in my own body as I am called to do. This agony is the agony of hell, of being cut off from the communion of persons.

On the other hand, if I, as a consecrated celibate, really begin to experience on earth even the beginnings of the intimate communion with God that I am called to live in heaven, then married sex is not necessary, for I have begun to experience not the shadow, but the very thing I am made for. Jesus told us that not all would be given the first tastes of this experience while on earth (Matthew 19:11), but some would be given it.

Now we can see why properly lived celibacy is a higher road. We now begin to understand why Teresa of Avila experienced hour-long ecstasies when she received Eucharist. Celibacy shows us where we are going. Marriage shows us how we get there.

Through marriage, we are united with a person made in the image and likeness of God, another human person who complements us, who completes us. With the grace God supplies through the sacrament, we practice treating each other as we would treat Christ, so that when we meet Christ, we can experience eternal ecstasy, more powerful than anything we have ever known.

Celibacy

Questions for discussion:

1) Compare and contrast what you knew about celibacy before reading reading this and after. What has changed?

2) Though celibacy for priests is only a discipline, do you think the discipline is likely to change?

3) Many parallels could be drawn between the Cross, the marriage bed, and Eucharistic adoration. How would you explain these connections to a friend?

4) This book makes no direct reference to chastity. However, given what you have read, how do you think chastity relates?

Scriptures for Contemplation

Matthew 19:10-12 - Jesus discusses marriage and celibacy

Mark 10:29-31 - Jesus discusses the rewards.

1 Corinthians 7:1-38 - Paul discusses marriage and celibacy

Catechism of the Catholic Church
Read and consider articles #437, 532, 915, 1579, 2348-2350

IX. Family Life

> The fecundity of conjugal love cannot be reduced solely
> to the procreation of children, but must extend to their
> moral education and their spiritual formation.
>
> *Catechism of the Catholic Church*, #2221

Up to this point, we have thought about how the theology of
the body changes our view of our spouse and of Christ. However,
we also need to think about how it changes our relationship towards
our children.

Remember, persons are defined by their relationships. As we
know, the key to understanding the Trinity is in understanding that
the divine relationships define the divine Persons. The Three Persons
are only distinguished by their relations. The divine relationships
are, in turn, characterized by total gift of Self in service to Another
and the total cooperation of each Person with the other Two: three
Persons with but one intellect, one will. Put another way, the three
Persons of the one God are of one mind and one heart.

Now, we are united to our spouse through the sacrament
of marriage, but we are also united to our children by that same
sacrament. For this reason, the teaching from the Catechism above is
well worth studying, for it contains within it the germ of everything
we need to see in order to better understand our lives as parents.
Let us begin with the phrase "conjugal love."

It is conjugal love, specifically, its physical expression in conjugal
relations, which creates not only the child, but also the parents and
their duties. This is a point worth dwelling on. We tend to think of
conception primarily in terms of child-creation, but that is really a
distorted understanding. Conception creates parents. Conception

creates parental duties. It creates parental rights. It creates the child. It creates the rights and duties of the child. All of this - the creation of the parents, parental rights and duties, the child and the child's rights and duties - are created at once, in the procreative act. But the opening statement describes even more. It points out that all of these creations - child, parent, rights and duties - are oriented towards a specific purpose.

> For Christian parents... the sacrament of marriage... consecrates them for the strictly Christian education of their children, that is to say, it calls upon them to share in the very authority and love of God the Father and Christ the Shepherd, and in the motherly love of the Church...

> By virtue of their ministry of educating... and by introducing them deeply through Christian initiation into the Body of Christ - both the Eucharistic and the ecclesial Body - [parents] become fully parents, in that they are begetters not only of bodily life but also of the life that through the Spirit's renewal flows from the Cross and Resurrection of Christ.
> John Paul II
> *Christian Family in the Modern World*, #38-39.

Take the chapter's opening statement together with this one, and we see a single statement being made. Physical begetting is only the beginning. Conjugal love is not fully life-giving until we parents show our children how to love and serve God. Only when the child learns who God is and how to love Him, only then do parents become fully parents. Only then have we fully begotten life within our own children.

We have seen how husband and wife are each Christ to the other, and how this is lived out in our bodies physically in the very act of married sexual intercourse. But now we must see how we also live out Christ's life in our own bodies in our relationship with our children. Jesus' three-year ministry of teaching and healing is the key to understanding this relationship. As parents, we are Christ to our children. We teach them by word and example. We lay down our lives in service to them. As Jesus walked among us, teaching and healing, so we walk among our children, teaching and healing. If this sounds somehow familiar, it should. The Gospel readings at every Mass are designed to teach as Christ taught, weaving together Old and New Testament readings to teach the baptized in preparation for their reception of the Bridegroom in Eucharist. First, we are taught by the Scripture, then we are healed by the Eucharist. What we do in our families is meant to imitate what happens at Mass every Sunday.

But all of this raises a further point. The sacrament of Holy Orders bears that name because the word "order" signifies a governing body. In Holy Orders, the priest becomes Christ for us. We already know that parents are Christ for their children. Thus, we should not be surprised to find that marriage consecrates the spouses into an *order*, a governing body, of the Church.

But the Church goes even farther than that. Thomas Aquinas pointed out that each family is a domestic Church. In a certain sense, marriage transforms husband and wife into priests, it makes our children our congregation. Our family images the sacred city. This is a startling way to look at marriage and children, but an even more startling conclusion can be drawn.

Because the family is the domestic church, we parents carry the responsibility to do what the Church does. The Church has three missions: to govern, to teach and to sanctify. These missions are intimately bound together:

...One can likewise speak of a right: from the
theological point of view every baptized person,
precisely by reason of being baptized, has the right
to receive from the Church instruction and education
enabling him or her to enter on a truly Christian life...
John Paul II
Catechesis in our Time, #14

Now, let us consider all these things together. Procreation is
our participation in the creation of an immortal person, a person
who will exist beyond time. But, says the opening paragraph to this
chapter, the life-giving quality of married love, that is, the life-giving
quality of sexual relations, cannot be reduced to just this. The act of
sex is an act that becomes fully life-giving only when the children
we conceive learn to love and serve the God who brought them
into existence through our human act.

Now, here's the startling part. We know that, properly lived,
conjugal life becomes in a certain sense liturgical. We can now also
see that moral education and spiritual formation is, in a certain
sense, also embedded in the sexual act. Consider: conjugal love
is expressed in the one-flesh union which is sex. Conception is a
natural consequence of the sexual expression of conjugal love. The
duty towards the moral education and spiritual formation of the
child is a natural consequence of the child's existence. When sex
is procreative, it simultaneously creates parents, child, rights and
duties. Among these rights and duties, the highest is the parental
duty to educate, and the child's right to be educated, in Christian
understanding. Conjugal love, sex, child, the right to Christian
education: each is a natural consequence so tightly intertwined

with what precedes it that they can together be considered a single entity: fecundity.

Earlier, we saw that sex between husband and wife is an image of the Eucharist. Now we see that sex between husband and wife also makes them an image of Christ the Teacher.

That's the positive aspect. But just as the connection between sex and Eucharist can be distorted by contraception, so the connection between sex and Christ the Teacher can also be distorted. The distortions are remarkably similar.

Pope Paul VI, in *Humanae Vitae* #14, described contraception in this way, "Every action which, either in anticipation of the conjugal act, or in its accomplishment, or *in the development of its natural consequences*, proposes, whether as an end or as a means, to render procreation impossible" (emphasis added).

We already know that moral education and spiritual formation are embedded in the sexual act; they are natural consequences of procreation. If we, as spouses - if we, as parents - do not fully engage ourselves in the Christian education of our children, we are refusing the full glory of our parenthood. Just as a man's service to his wife helps her reach her perfection, and he reaches his own perfection through his service to her, so a father's service to his own children - specifically his instruction of his own children in the Faith - is also necessary for his perfection.

> The *role of parents in education* is of such importance that it is almost impossible to provide an adequate substitute. (emphasis in the original)
> Vatican Council II,
> *Declaration on Christian Education*, #3

At Vatican II, the Holy Spirit said the parental role in education is almost impossible to replace. Shortly after Vatican II, Pope Paul VI described contraception as an interference with natural consequences which renders procreation impossible. Education is a natural consequence of procreation, the giving of life. Without parental involvement, it is nearly impossible to give children the life of grace. There is a deep resonance between openness to life, the rejection of contraception, and openness to actively teaching our own children, the rejection of passivity in our child's Faith formation.

Do we need to teach the entire Faith to them ourselves? No. We need to be involved in that aspect of Faith formation which directly propagates life. As a married couple, by the very fact that we have sex, we have sworn with our bodies that we will "initiate our children at an early age into the mysteries of the faith..." as article 2225 in the *Catechism of the Catholic Church* says.

But, what are the mysteries of the faith? The *Catechism of the Catholic Church* is divided into four major sections. Look at the title to Part II: "The Celebration of the Christian Mystery." What is that entire section about? The sacraments. Indeed, in the Eastern Church, the very word for "sacrament" is "mysterion" - mystery. Just as the sperm and egg are the source of biological life, the sacraments are the source of spiritual life. So, the act of sex between husband and wife creates in us, as husband and wife, the responsibility to prepare our own children for the sacraments. We become fully parents when we give our children the fullness of life, both biological and spiritual.

This is something most parents don't realize. Sacramental preparation of children is, in the last analysis, not primarily the bishop's job, nor the priest's task, nor the DRE's responsibility, nor the CCD teacher's work. Sacramental preparation is our job, our task, our responsibility, our work, as parents. It is our vocation. The bishop is there to help us, the priest will assist us, the DRE may set up classes so that we can learn how to do it well, the CCD teacher will instruct our children in supporting skills and supporting knowledge, but the glory of sacramental initiation is really ours. We are supposed to prepare our own children for First Reconciliation, Confirmation and First Eucharist. We bear that responsibility because we create and bear the children.

There are many who find the Theology of the Body controversial in various ways, in its frank talk about sex, about the human body, about the connections between the practices of the Church and the practices of the bedroom. But it is in this consequence, a consequence nearly unnoticed by most of those who discuss this understanding of the Faith, that the real controversy is found.

When we approach the altar to be married, we are not just marrying that beautiful woman or handsome man of our dreams. We are also being ordained, we are being consecrated, as catechists. In order to fulfill this aspect of our service to our family, we must ourselves be well-instructed in the Faith and we must be willing to initiate our children into the Christian mysteries. Most of us aren't. We have neither the knowledge nor the courage to do this most frightening thing, the thing for which sex was created. Sex exists not only so that we might live out the life of the Trinity in our own bodies, but so that we might live out the mission of the Trinity in our own lives: to create new persons and bring those new persons into the full glory of their personhood through knowledge of and relationship with God.

Sex in the Sacred City of marriage is meant to glorify God not only in the beauty of the sexual act itself, but ultimately in the staggering reality it creates: a new, eternally-existing person who is given life through the sacraments on earth and through life with God in heaven. Forget about dangerous sexually transmitted diseases and delicate books on sexual technique - this is the most dangerous and delicate aspect of sex: to procreate and properly instruct our own children in the Faith.

What would you do if the pastor of your parish stood at the ambo next Sunday and informed the parish that all sacramental preparation would henceforth be done by the parents? The parish would offer classes and instruction to assist the parents in their work. The pastor or his delegate, as required by canon law, would verify the child's readiness for the sacrament when the parents presented the child as a candidate, but sacramental preparation would be done entirely - or at least mainly - by the parents and no one else. Parish religion classes for children would deal with the supporting aspects of religious instruction, such as familiarity with Scripture and learning common prayers, but most CCD classes would now be designed to help the priests of the domestic Church prepare their own children for First Reconciliation, Confirmation and First Eucharist. These domestic priests, the parents, would become fully parents by performing the necessary instruction for their congregation, their children.

How many of us would be prepared to accept the challenge? If a pastor were to make such an announcement, he would be doing exactly what the Church demands of him as pastor and we would be doing exactly what is demanded of us as parents. Bishops are the first catechists of the diocese, but parents are the primary educators of their own children. Priests are the first catechists of their parish, but they are merely assistants to the parents when it comes to the instruction of the parents' own children. The Church herself has always taught this:

> The Bishops ensure that the authentic Catholic faith is transmitted to parents so that they, in turn, can pass it on to their children. Teachers and educators at all levels also assist in this process. The laity bear witness to that purity of faith which Bishops take pains to maintain. It is important that each Bishop endeavor to provide the laity with the means for a suitable formation through centres set up for this purpose.
> *World Synod Document on Bishops and the Ministry of the Word*, 2001, #105

We parents are the primary educators of our own children. We are the first educators. We are the ones who are called on to initiate our children into the mysteries of the faith. When I confer the sacrament of marriage upon my wife, and my wife confers the sacrament of marriage upon me, with the priest and the congregation standing near as witnesses, we publicly state our willingness to do exactly what this hypothetical priest proposes.

Is such a scenario frightening? If it isn't, it should be. It is an unspeakably great responsibility. But it is also the greatest act of love we could ever show towards our children. Love is frightening - it calls forth tremendous sacrifice. Children not only have a right to know about God, they have a right to learn the intimate love of God from their parents, in the context of their own family. As spouses, by the very fact of our sexual union, we have sworn with our bodies that we will be and do exactly that.

Questions for discussion:

1) Discuss the implications of the phrase "Parents are priests of the domestic Church."

2) Given that Jesus is God, how could Mary and Joseph fully live out their role as parents in the Holy Family? What could they teach God?

3) Draw up a list of the things you think a child might need to know in order to be properly prepared for First Reconciliation, First Eucharist and Confirmation. Have each list checked by a priest or deacon. How would you go about instructing your child in these mysteries of the Faith?

4) In order to explain something to children, we typically need to understand it at an adult level first. What books or tapes might you investigate in order to grow in your own understanding?

Scriptures for Contemplation

Luke 2:40-52 - Mary and Joseph in their relationship with Jesus.

Ephesians 6:1-4 - Instructions for fathers.

1 Tim 5:1-5 - Instructions for family relations.

Catechism of the Catholic Church
Read and consider articles #1652-1658, 2201-2233

Conclusion

> One of the urgent needs of our time… is attention to families since they are experiencing "a radical and widespread crisis" because of the serious threats that beset them today: the breakup of marriages, the scourge of abortion, the contraceptive mentality, moral corruption, infidelity and violence in the home, factors that endanger the family, which is the primary cell of society and of the Church.
>
> Pope John Paul II
> General audience, Nov 23, 2001

We conclude with this quote because with it we have accomplished what we set out to do. We have studied the entirety of Church teaching through the perspective that has guided the Church for two millenia.

You may reply in amazement, "But how can this be? We have discussed very little in this short space."

"On the contrary," I would reply, "We have discussed the necessary things from the necessary perspective."

Consider. We now have a much more thorough understanding of Trinity - who God is in Himself. We needed to know this because God is both our source and our goal - we came from Him and we are meant to return to Him. Everything that improves our understanding of Trinity is worth its weight in grace.

We have a clearer understanding of what we are called to. We are called to love, that is, we are called to serve others with everything we are.

We are called into one-flesh communion with the divine Person of Christ, either alone, through the living Christ present in the

Eucharist, or through the combination of Eucharist and the living Christ who is our spouse.

We have discovered that marriage is the source of our salvation, it is the mystery which must be understood in order to fully understand Christ the Bridegroom and His Bride, His Body, the Church.

We know marriage must be fecund. We know that fecundity is not just the gift of biological life, but the gift of spiritual life as well, and that we, as parents, become fully parents only when we fully participate in giving spiritual life to our children.

God gave us both biological and spiritual life. We know that when we are fully fecund, we live out God's life in our own bodies.

We know that living married life well sanctifies the world and makes us like unto God. It prepares us for life in heaven because it gives us the opportunity to practice living heaven on earth. Through married life, we live a foretaste of heaven's sacred city.

We know that life in heaven is perfect, intimate, bodily communion with God, the First Family of Persons, through our baptismal and Eucharistic union with Christ, our Bridegroom.

And in this last quote, the Holy Father summarizes all of these ideas in a single phrase: "the family... is the primary cell of society and of the Church." Family life is the foundation for everything. If every family lives its life in imitation of the Trinity, human society will be healed, the virgin Church will be perfected. If families do not live this life out, society will continue to disintegrate, the Church will continue to suffer the effects of that disintegration in her members.

A family can only live the life of the Trinity when both the mother and the father are dedicated to living the divine vision. "A mother's dedication to her home and her children is the loftiest role she can carry out. Without the mother, there is no home, no family, no country, even no Church!" exclaimed the Holy Father to a group of bishops in February, 1995. Similarly, in the Scripture quote with which we started this volume, "I bow my knee before the Father, from whom every family in heaven and on earth is named," the Greek word for "family" is *patria,* which literally means "fatherhood."

And so we end with the Holy Father's exhortation to us, the married couples, who have sex and seek the Sacred City, who have children and teach them to seek the Sacred City:

"Christian Families, Become What You Are!"

About the Author

Steve Kellmeyer is a popular Catholic author and lecturer who has written hundreds of articles for Catholic newspapers, magazines and websites. His work has appeared in *National Catholic Register*, *This Rock*, *Envoy*, *Lay Witness*, *Homiletics & Pastoral Review*, *The Catholic Answer*, *Social Justice Review* and *The New Oxford Review*. He has also appeared on *The Total Living Network with Jerry Rose* and on the Pax TV special, *Breaking the Da Vinci Code*.

Designed to Fail, the book whose opening chapter follows this page, expands on the meditation on family life found in this book. Using the same thoughtful analysis of Magisterial documents, Kellmeyer shows how the American parochial school system inadvertently violates the theology of the body. Indeed, as Kellmeyer demonstrates in his other books, John Paul II's vision answers not only the problem of parochial education, but a wide range of problems, from the concerns created by *The Da Vinci Code* to the detailed Scriptural defense of Catholic doctrine and everything in between.

Holding an MA in catechetical theology from Franciscan University, Steubenville and an MA in modern European history from Southern Illinois University, Edwardsville, Steve Kellmeyer also has undergraduate degrees in computer science, medical laboratory technology and math education. He has worked or published in every field in which he holds a degree.

An outstanding speaker who skillfully shows how theology applies to today's headlines, he appears frequently in lecture halls and on radio stations both across the nation and internationally. He resides in Peoria, Ilinois with his bride, Veronica, and their children.

Bonus

Designed to Fail:
Catholic Education in America

Chapter 1

Chapter 1: The Incarnation to Trent

The Example of Scripture

> Then were little children presented to him, that he should impose hands upon them and pray. And the disciples rebuked them. But Jesus said to them: "Suffer the little children, and forbid them not to come to me: for the kingdom of heaven is for such." And when he had imposed hands upon them, he departed from thence. *

Start a conversation on Catholic schools in America today and someone will invariably bring that passage up with a look of heartfelt passion. Many seem to assume it forms part of the divine mandate which authorizes the Church to teach children. It doesn't.**
In fact, if the passage demonstrates anything, it demonstrates that Jesus didn't teach children. Instead, He focused like a laser on adults. The Gospel of Matthew describes the events in the third and last year of Jesus' ministry. He apparently focused so strongly on instructing adults in the Faith that when children were brought to His apostles, these same apostles - having had two full years of training with the Master - told the children to go away. They had never seen Jesus involve Himself with healthy children.

Imagine the apostolic shock when Jesus, apparently for the first time since they had met Him, took a few moments off from teaching adults to pray over children and impose His hands upon them. But notice something else: He did not teach those children. Matthew is very clear on this. Instead, as soon as He had finished praying over them, He left. In the very next verse, He has returned to teaching adults.

Many would consider the above interpretation of the Scripture passage absurd, but they fail to notice the context of the passage. To begin with, it is embedded in the Gospels. One may say many

---

* Matthew 19:13-15.
** The authority to teach actually comes from the Great Commission of Matthew 28:18-20.

things about the Gospels, but one may not say that they are anything other than distinctly adult books. Indeed, the same is true of every book of Scripture. The Pauline letters carry no children's illustrations. Peter's letter, written for adults, tells us Scripture is hard to understand and easily twisted: in short, not recommended for children. The Old Testament liturgies, laws and prophecies are complex, detailed and require a broad acquaintance with the whole of Scripture and adult life. Animals are slaughtered wholesale and retail, war and illicit sex abound, of a children's Passover there is no hint. We too easily forget that children's Bibles are created only through enormous expurgation. The divinely inspired prophets wrote for adults.

From all the historical evidence, the Apostles, personally trained by God Himself, seem as oblivious to teaching children as the divinely inspired prophets of old. Even the most cursory reading of the Acts of the Apostles demonstrates this. Not one of the men personally chosen, trained and ordained by God looked out on the vast pagan world that jostled about them and said, "Well, the adults around here are thoroughly pagan and definitely past saving. They won't come to hear our sermons. If we are to succeed in passing on the Faith, we must work on the next generation – the children. Let's start a parochial school." That alone is instructive.

The Examples of the Fathers and Doctors

But the divine example does not end there. Not only did the prophets never instruct children directly, not only does Jesus never instruct children directly, not only did the twelve apostles fail to start parochial schools, but the men personally trained by the Twelve also failed to see the instruction of children as the key to transmitting the Faith. None of the early bishops seemed to have directly involved themselves in the training of children. This is most remarkable, especially when we take into account another relevant fact, that of infant baptism:

> As to what pertains to the case of infants: You [Fidus] said that they ought not to be baptized within the second or third day after their birth, that the old law of circumcision must be taken into consideration, and that you did not think that one should be baptized and sanctified within the eighth day after his birth. In our council it seemed to us far otherwise. No one agreed to the course which you thought should be taken. Rather, we all judge that the mercy and grace of God ought to be denied to no man born.*

Although Cyprian insists on the earliest possible baptism, this Father of the Church does not appear to have started a single school of instruction for the children he baptized. Irenaeus, Hippolytus, Origen, Gregory of Nazianzen, John Chrysostom, Augustine, the Fifth Council of Carthage and the Second Council of Mileum – all insisted on infant baptism, but not one appears to have started or even mentioned elementary schools.

At this point, the alert reader might reply that this is not entirely accurate. Did not St. John Chrysostom say, "What greater work is there than training the mind and forming the habits of the young?"** Indeed he did. But the Latin reads "Ouid maius quam animis moderari, quam *adolescentulorum* fingere mores?" (emphasis added). That is, Chrysostom was referring to the education of teenagers. This is quite clear from the context of the homily in which the sentence appears, a homily in which the saint is at pains to point out:

> The fathers are to blame. They require their horse-breakers to discipline their horses, they do not permit the colt to remain untamed. Instead, they put a rein and all the rest upon it from the beginnings. But their children? These they overlook. They allow their children to go about for a long season unbridled, and without temperance, disgracing themselves by fornications and

---

* Cyprian of Carthage, *Letters* 64:2 [A.D. 253]).
** Homily #59 on Matthew 18.

gamings and attending the wicked theaters. Before the fornication began, they should have given their son to a wife, to a wife chaste, and highly endowed with wisdom. Such a wife will bring her husband away from this disorderly course of life, and will be instead a rein to the colt…. Do you not know that you can do no greater kindness to a youth than to keep him pure from whorish uncleanness?*

But Chrysostom does not stop there. In this same homily, he also points out that many people are giving the wrong reading to Matthew 18:10, and he intends to put them straight:

> [The Gospel says] take heed that ye despise not one of these little ones; for I say unto you, that their angels do always behold the face of my Father which is in Heaven" (Matthew 18:10). By the phrase "little ones" He does not mean those who are really little. Rather, He means those who everyone considers useless: the poor, the contemptible, the unknown – these are called little, but they are equal in value to the whole world, they are called little who are dear to God. But no one among us thinks of them in this way. **

Chrysostom is not alone in this reading. Origen, Jerome, Hilary, Remigius and even Aquinas, writing a millennium later, give essentially identical interpretations of Matthew 18:10. Again, we may hear the complaint that Aquinas, near the end of his life, loved best to train children to receive the Eucharist. True, to a point. The reception of First Eucharist during Aquinas' life was typically twelve to fifteen years of age – Aquinas was training what we would consider teens, but what he would consider young adults.

During Aquinas' life, marriage at the age of 16 was not uncommon, death by 45, typical. As we shall see later in this book, agrarian societies considered anyone twelve or older essentially an adult. Such a person was expected to act like an adult and

* ibid.
** ibid.

thus generally did so. This puts rather a different perspective on things. We are now beginning to see that none of these Fathers and Doctors of the Church addressed the problem of elementary school education. They poured all of their energies into teaching adults.

While the Church did establish schools in the first century, these schools were almost invariably for adults, not children. They were intended to train Christian philosophers to answer the objections brought by pagan philosophers against Christian doctrine. No council mentions the need to train children in the Faith until the Council of Vaison in 529 A.D. – that's half a millennium after Jesus rose from the dead. Even then, the directive was only towards the training of boys in the liturgy and the Scriptures, that is, the Council was primarily interested in training young men for the clerical life.

But how can this be? After all, once a person is baptized, that person has the right to receive instruction in the Faith. The Church has a duty to instruct the baptized in the Faith, a duty to impart all and everything the Catholic Church knows to the baptized. Indeed, the Church has only three missions in this world: to govern, to teach, and to sanctify. Baptism not only sanctifies, it creates the obligation to teach the one sanctified. Why would Apostles, Fathers, Doctors, even Councils of the Church insist on infant baptism yet be so marvelously, immovably silent concerning the establishment of schools of instruction for those same baptized youth?

How Christian children were trained

It may be hard to believe, but for at least the first five centuries Christian children were educated in the Faith exclusively at home. While none of the Fathers and Doctors of the Church mention elementary schools, many comment on the importance of mothers in passing on the Faith, beginning with Paul himself.[*] Mothers such as Macrina, Emmelia, Nonna, Anthusa, Monica, and Paula, mothers of saints and scholars, show the success of Christian homeschooling against pagan influence and pagan schools.

---

* 2 Timothy 1:5.

For the first twelve centuries of Church history, the sacramental preparation of children was not an issue. Baptism, Confirmation and first Eucharist, via the Precious Blood, were all delivered to the infant in a single ceremony shortly after birth. Thus, sacramental preparation of children in today's sense of the word was both unnecessary and unknown. Pagan children who were very young were simply baptized, confirmed and given the Eucharist as any infant would be. If they were old enough to understand the content of adult instruction, they would be included with the adults who were being instructed in the Faith. These adults were also baptized, confirmed and given First Eucharist in that order in a single Easter Vigil ceremony. There were no separate instructional processes for children. Sacramental instruction was a unitive whole.

Every baptized child's education in the Faith was exclusively the task of the parent. This is why Jesus prays for the children, but does not teach them – that was the parents' duty. The Twelve preach to adults but not to children – that was the parents' duty. In the first millennium of the Church, schools were established primarily to train adults or to form priests, but they were generally not established to pass the Faith onto Christian children – that was the parents' duty.

True, by John Chrysostom's time (380's A.D.), parents were already beginning to fail in this duty. Chrysostom laments the fact that parents no longer took seriously the task God had ordained them to do. But even though Chrysostom notes the fact, he does not take it upon himself to step into the breach and provide elementary schools, nor does he delegate any of his priests or deacons to do so. Instead, he simply continues to teach the parents, and exhort them to do their duty.

Early Mission Schools
This is, of course, not the entire story. There were a few attempts to set up elementary schools early on. In about 372 A.D., for instance, a Christian named Protogenes, who had been denounced for holding the Faith, was exiled to the town of Edessa, on the

right bank of the Nile. Upon reaching the town, he discovered that most of the inhabitants were pagans. So, with the local bishop's permission, he set up a school for pagan children, teaching them to read the Psalms and the Gospels. When one boy fell sick, he healed him through prayer. As others fell sick, parents brought their children to him for healing. He refused to pray for the children unless the parents agreed to baptize them. While the school seems to have been successful, its existence also seems to have ended when his exile ended and he was allowed to return home.

Another recorded attempt to set up an elementary school did not go quite so well. After Julian the Apostate, the anti-Catholic Emperor of Rome, forced the bishop Saint Cassian to flee his episcopal see in 363 AD, Cassian established a school for training pagan boys. He wanted to teach them about Christ by first teaching them to read and write. Yet, within a year of the school's founding, his educational plan was interrupted when he was denounced as a Christian. His punishment? He was turned over to the pagan students he had been teaching. The students promptly showed their love of elementary education by stabbing the bishop with their iron styluses and breaking their slates over his head. None of the children proved able to deal a killing blow, however, so Cassian bled to death in his classroom over the course of hours.

The story of his martyrdom is not one of elementary education's success stories, but it is instructive. Notice that these elementary schools were set up exclusively to teach pagan children. They were mission schools. There is no mention of teaching the baptized in such schools. Notice also that the bishop with whom Protogenes worked had not been running even a mission school for pagan children and he does not seem to have been much interested in the enterprise.

Organization of the Christian School

Now, as time went on, schools to train young men for priesthood and for monastic life were established. The importance of the monasteries in reference to Christian learning cannot be overemphasized. There were no parishes in the early church. Each city had its own bishop and the cathedral was often the only church building in town. While the country-folk might be associated with a particular city, they would typically find their spiritual life most thoroughly satisfied through contact with the monastic communities in the countryside. They would hear the bells of the monastery calling the monks to prayer. The monks were the closest source of healing sacraments. Their manual labour made the surrounding area safe for human habitation as they cleared impenetrable forests and drained swamps. Since the vast majority of people in agrarian societies lived in the country, monasteries were key to the transmission of adult Catholic Faith.*

These adult monastic communities served the spiritual needs of their neighbors. Eventually, as adults inquired about living the monastic life, the monasteries found it useful to create schools of instruction for those who wanted to join the community. As these schools grew over the centuries, they began to take in other Christian students, students who clearly did not intend to take up religious life. Still, as we shall see, this latter tendency grew slowly. It isn't until the ninth and tenth centuries that we begin to see a reliable distinction being made between students who are being trained for religious life and students who are being trained for secular life.

In the monastic schools established for Christian instruction, the curriculum commonly revolved around seven subjects: the "trivium" of grammar, logic** and rhetoric, and the "quadrivium" of arithmetic, geometry, astronomy, and music. Both groupings were intended to serve a larger purpose. Grammar provided the introduction to literature, the study of how adults wrote to and

---

* As Fr. Joseph Fessio pointed out at the 1996 Wanderer Forum, 14th century Europe had 15,000 monasteries in a population of 75 million. To reach a comparable density of monasteries today, each and every U.S. diocese would need roughly 300 monasteries.
** Sometimes also called dialectic.

about other adults concerning adult issues. Logic studied how to construct formal arguments, how to build a set of concepts towards a coherent whole. It involved dialectic, the study of how to resolve disagreements that arose from logic. Rhetoric discussed basic law and history, necessary for the study of philosophical and metaphysical concepts.

So, grammar provided the basic vocabulary of the adult world. Logic/dialectic showed how those adult concepts and virtues tied together and had been lived out in the past. Rhetoric discussed the general theory of virtuous living. Together, the three described how man should live in the world.

The higher studies, that is, the disciplines suitable for "high school," included the quadrivium of arithmetic, geometry, music, and astronomy. Together, these described the physical world in much the same way the trivium described the life of the adult. Arithmetic was not just addition and subtraction, it included basic statistics, number theory and logic. Numbers were, in a sense, the grammar, the language, of the physical world. Geometry applied Euclid's elements, and thus could include things like geography and surveying. It was the logic of the physical world; it showed how the pieces of the physical world fit together. Astronomy laid the foundation for physics and advanced mathematics; it described the physical movement of the cosmos. Music discussed both theory and practice; since the planets were believed to produce music as the angels moved them, music was the language of the cosmos.* The quadrivium taught the student how to think of the earth beneath his feet and the sky above his head – the whole universe outside himself.

Together, the trivium and the quadrivium described every aspect of the known world, both spiritual and physical, the inner man and the world through which he moved. Once this training was completed, the student had a firm understanding both of the world and of his place in it. Christian education rounded these

---

* Gustav Holst's symphony *The Planets* recalls this understanding.

seven subjects out with theology, the eighth subject that suffused every subject. It was the goal for which the first seven subjects prepared a man. In short, theology, God's plan for man's salvation, tied it all together in a coherent whole.

> We sent our three children to Catholic grade school for three months. The textbooks were books used by the state schools (we are in Texas) and were very secular. We didn't feel that our children were receiving a Catholic education. In fact, at this point, we don't even know what a "Catholic education" truly means... We now home school our children to be certain they receive proper instruction and strong academics. We were very disappointed with our brief Catholic school experience because we do not feel that our school, which has been around for nearly 60 years, is Catholic in its fundamental teachings. Things must have changed. – *email from Texas*

The Problem of Literacy

As the schools grew, they needed regulation. The Third Lateran Council (1179) required "[I]n order that the opportunity of learning to read and progress in study is not withdrawn from poor children who cannot be helped by the support of their parents, in every cathedral church a master is to be assigned some proper benefice so that he may teach the clerics of that church and the poor scholars."* By that time, entire clerical communities, such as the Brothers of the Common Life, were being founded expressly to be educators. Schools continued to grow. By the late 1300's, the number and variety of schools was rather impressive: monastic schools, cathedral schools, canonicate schools, chantry schools,

---

* Third Lateran Council,18th decree.

guild schools, hospital schools, city schools, and special educational institutions.

Even so, literacy was a skill as common to medieval populations as airplane piloting is a skill common to our own. The reason is simple. Flying a plane is a wonderfully useful skill if you can afford to own one. Before the advent of the printing press, books were as expensive as private planes are today. The vellum and parchment for the pages required calf, kid or lamb-skin – lots of it. A single book represented the slaughter of an entire herd, something only a wealthy man could afford. Once the skins were obtained, each skin had to go through long chemical preparation before being converted by careful scraping. Once that was done, monastic scriveners could spend weeks, months or years copying out the complete work by hand and illustrating the pages. Finally, a suitably rich protective cover, not uncommonly embossed in gold or encrusted with jewels, had to be produced to protect the new and precious item. Covers were sometimes so rich that thieves would rip out and leave behind the vellum pages of a book just to get the cover.

So unless a king supported the training of literate men, there was little way to finance it. In a subsistence society, the time and energy it took for small communities to train large numbers of people in a little-used skill that didn't directly contribute to feeding and clothing that community was an expense few could afford. Thus, while schools grew in number, most schools were oriented towards producing the biggest bang for their buck: priests. Since priests mediated the sacraments of salvation, it was crucial that they understood what they were doing in the liturgy. Salvation came first.

Monks were trained to read and write because they had to know the Scriptures and the liturgy. They were supposed to guard and maintain these holy things as they assisted a person towards heaven. As the advantages of literacy to management became clear, kings who were themselves illiterate would employ monks to help them manage far-flung holdings, much in the same way that today's

CEO's hire computer people, and for much the same reason. We may understand how rarely lay people were trained in literacy skills by simply considering the name we still give to management support staff. To this day, we hire "clerical" staff. Why? Because the secretaries to royalty were always men consecrated through the sacrament of Holy Orders. They were clerics.

When we consider the expense of books and thus the expense of education in general, we can see why so little attention was paid to specialized curricula for children. Even rich men could rarely afford to train themselves or their retinue in literacy skills. Children could not be secretaries and advisors to kings. A child who might one day rule would be trained in the art of literacy, but only because someone who had money sponsored the child.

Thus, when the Lateran Council insisted that even the poor be taught, it said this in reference to training for the priesthood – after all, the poor are as legitimately called to Holy Orders as the rich. No one who wished to discern the priesthood would be turned away simply on account of poverty. The Church provided the only real path for upward economic mobility in Europe if only because she made no distinction between peasants and princes. She assisted both on a daily basis.

During this time, the idea of children's books was, of course, completely absurd. Schools taught adults by lecture for the simple reason that the only one who might have a book was the teacher. If students had the vellum, the pen and the literacy skills, they were expected to create their own books by copying down what the lecturer said word for word as he read from and commented on his own book. At the end of the course, all the students would then have a text to keep and refer to for the remainder of their lives. It was a far cry from a modern publishing house, but given the circumstances, it was the best anyone could do.

Early Changes in Education

Two things changed the state of education. First, the rapidly growing Christian population quickly outstripped the number of bishops available to administer Confirmation. As a result, while infants could be baptized, they were not being confirmed. Indeed, Confirmation was often delayed for years at a time. Since the Church insisted that the sacraments should be received in order - Baptism, Confirmation, then Eucharist - reception of the Eucharist was also pushed back. By the time of Thomas Aquinas, the reception of these last two sacraments had been pushed so far back that the young needed to go through a specific post-baptismal instructional period.

The reason for this is simple: when we receive a sacrament, we must give everything we are to Christ. At baptism, the infant does this through the gift the parents make of him to God. The infant cannot choose for himself. He is under the authority of his parents, so his parents choose for him. But, once a person gains the use of reason, he must personally choose to give himself to God. Of course, in order to do that, the person has to know what it is he is choosing. Thus, a person who has the use of reason must be instructed before sacramental reception in a way that an infant need not be. Sacramental instruction of baptized youth was an innovation made necessary due to the relative absence of bishops.

The second change was more prosaic. In 1450, the printing press was invented.* Within a few short years, the price of a book dropped to two percent of its former value. Forty years after Gutenburg set ink to press, America was discovered. Twenty-five years after that

---

* The Chinese invented paper in 200 BC, and its use spread to the Middle East by the 10th century. Unfortunately, the Middle East was controlled by Islam. Though paper was known to Christian Europe by the 12th century, it was not widely used, since it was seen as a Moslem invention and the Moslems had cut Christians off from the Holy Lands. The First Crusade had retaken Jerusalem and re-established the pilgrimage routes, but all the gains were lost by 1200. So, by 1221, Holy Roman Emperor Frederick II decreed that any legal document written on paper was invalid. It was not until the printing press created astronomical demand for printing materials that paper became common throughout Europe.

discovery, Luther hammered 95 theses to the cathedral door in Wittenburg. America and Europe would together ride the crest of the explosion in books and literacy that Catholics had created.

> The thought has crossed our mind before about closing down the parish schools for a year or two to focus on adult education and then reopening with a more solid adult foundation in place. A practical solution? Absolutely not. Something that will ever happen? Unlikely. Yet at the same time, to even have that thought crossing our minds is an indication of the desperate straits Catholic education finds itself in. - *email from Illinois*

The rest of Chapter 1, along with the whole remarkable story of American Catholic education, can be found in:

Designed to Fail: Catholic Education in America

Available through Bridegroom Press

www.bridegroompress.com

Get the Catholic Perspective!